MANHATTAN
PEOPLE AND THEIR SPACE

DATE			
7/18/96			
12/9/02			

© THE BAKER & TAYLOR CO.

MANHATTAN
PEOPLE AND THEIR SPACE

Roberte Mestdagh

with 55 illustrations and map

THAMES AND HUDSON

◁ **TITLE PAGE: Sky, from a roof at 119th Street, looking northeast.**

© Roberte Mestdagh 1981

First published in 1981 by Thames and Hudson Ltd, London

First published in the USA in 1982 by Thames and Hudson Inc., 500 Fifth Avenue, New York, New York 10110

Library of Congress Catalog card number: 81–52751

Printed and bound in Great Britain by W. Clowes (Beccles) Ltd.

Contents

PUBLISHER'S NOTE

The sequence and positioning of the photographs reflect the viewpoint of a person making a circuit around Manhattan. The route begins on the Upper East Side, proceeds south to the lower tip of Manhattan, and then turns north via the West Side to Harlem. Photographs are oriented to convey the perspectives of a traveler following this itinerary.

Introduction

The shapes and the gaps of a city limit our field of vision and define our possibilities of travel and movement. The space is the place for the actions of the people and through it we penetrate into the rhythm and the pace of an urban milieu. We participate in it through our own attitudes and by the feelings we project into it.

The city as a structure created by man reflects the thought pattern of a society, its notions of space and time. There is a constant interaction between a place and its inhabitants.

This complementary relationship between mental space and physical space can manifest itself in the daily life of those who live in urban surroundings. For this purpose, I chose to interview inhabitants of Manhattan. Manhattan has so little natural scenery that it is almost entirely the product of man. The vertical universe of Midtown, symbol of our western civilization, both unique and extreme, allows the effect of the environment on people to be plainly highlighted, just as the relationship of time and space. On this island, a multitude of ethnic and cultural communities live side by side, some of them in clearly delimited territories. This offers a vast field of comparison between the different reactions to the urban milieu.

I met eighty-one people from different groups. The flexibility of my questions varied according to the contact established, the specific problems of each ethnic or cultural group, each individual. Certain communities are lacking, certain districts are not totally represented. The aim was not to give a detailed view of Manhattan, but to bring out as much as possible the influence of this city on its inhabitants. The eighteen texts selected are transcriptions of the most significant interviews from each of the communities approached.

The photos situate the people in their surroundings, give the relationship of the neighborhood to the sky and to the vertical. They connect the texts with one another and make up a journey through Manhattan.

The photo-montages give a view of the place which the eye does not perceive as a whole in one moment. The 360° horizontal views were taken by turning around on the spot and putting together the series of photos taken one after another. The 360° vertical views are series of photos taken from the ground upwards, making one complete round. The four photo-montages of the East Side are views taken in the middle of the crossroads and inserted into the plan of Manhattan.

The eye – and *a fortiori* the camera – gives only a limited view of the place, and yet what affects us is the whole.

It is by considering all the factors composing the life of an individual that one can understand the different approaches to an environment and the whys and wherefores of these differences.

360° horizontal view from the top of the Empire State Building.

Crossing 96th Street

Silvia

33, beauty consultant; born Westchester County; lives in Harlem.

Driving down Fifth Avenue from Harlem to Upper East Side
. . . You have a lot of Puerto Ricans in this area. Not right on Fifth Avenue—you got to go across Park Avenue before you see Puerto Ricans.
. . . You see how they're tearing down these buildings? But these are good buildings that no way should have been taken down. They're burning all over. Fire trucks, you hear them all night long in Harlem and the South Bronx. . . . Now these are projects, all this is City housing. They're burning the old buildings and they build this. They burn on one side and they build on the other side.
. . . You never heard of the crossing of 110th Street? You just crossed over 110th Street. But these days it is the same when you cross 96th Street, because this is low income too. The two different worlds—now you're coming to the glorified section of Manhattan.
. . . This is a very well-known hospital, Mount Sinai Hospital. They have a habit of tearing down buildings or trying to get people out of their apartments. You can't even live in the neighborhood because they're bringing in interns and doctors to live there.
. . . Now you are into money. This is money here. All these buildings are co-op. Now you are with the doorman service, things like that. The two worlds.

I like people, I wouldn't live down here. They have to be unhappy people if they spend a lot of money to go somewhere else to have fun. I came to work yesterday, Sunday—deserted. At 7:30 there are a lot of people and at 10 o'clock at night there is nobody around. I come down here ten to six, Monday to Friday, for one thing: to get the paycheck. So my eyes are on two places, the restaurant across the street, because that's where I have my breakfast, and the building where I work on Park Avenue. I see nothing else. But when I go home I like to see everything, because Harlem fascinates me, because there is always something different, always something going on up there, and I love it. I can go and join in if I want, I can sit on the side, and no one is saying, "What are you looking at?" And I am respected more in that community. I feel protected, I feel safe, very safe.
   The street I live on is nice because New York City just made it an historical area. There is this old church that has been there for one hundred years, and

by living right across the street from it we benefit. So our street is very clean, very well kept, we have trees. And the people in the street are nice. We have a ten-room brownstone. It was a very good deal, we got the house for a fantastic price. Once you buy a home, you think about it differently than if you were renting it. So you try to get your neighbors doing what you are doing, and then you get your friends into the neighborhood. You're kind of building your own community. If you can get one person like that on each block in Harlem, I think it could turn the whole thing around. My view is that New York City doesn't want to get the educated blacks back there because then they're going to have a little problem on their hands. And this is my goal, to give them a little problem and to show them they are no longer going to pussyfoot around with our money. Our buying power is fantastic. If we stop bringing our money down here to buy in their stores, if we open our own stores right there in Harlem, we will crush New York. But the majority of stores in the area are still white-owned and that irritates me. So my hope is to get blacks to open their own business, get them into politics, get them to put on the pressure, get them the voting power.

I grew up in Westchester County in a typical suburb, about thirty minutes from here on the train. I come from the trees and the grass. It was a happy life. I wasn't brought up to be aware of race, and also I had mixed parents: my father was white, hispanic, my mother was black.

I remember when I was a little girl my grandfather lived in Harlem, on 118th Street, which is considered not such a good area to live. I couldn't wait to come down there. Harlem has always fascinated me. It fascinates me how many people can stand on one block at midday—people who are on welfare, people who are educated with good jobs, people who just have mediocre jobs, people who have interests outside the community, people whose main interest is in the one block they live in. But you have them all living together and they're not fighting one another. The first warm day, everybody will come out of the house.

Recreation to many people in Harlem is seeing their friends on the streets, going to church. We have more churches in Harlem than any other place—that's our recreation. Unfortunately, the city doesn't bring proper recreation to Harlem because everyone is afraid. People hear about this one who was killed and they think Harlem is a bad place. They refuse to loosen up and say, "Well, this place has to be like every other place, there are crimes every-where." The news media haven't been too nice about it. When they have a story about Harlem it's always about the deterioration. But they have failed to realize that all these burning houses . . . it's because the white landlords want us out of Harlem.

The state buildings are the only high buildings in Harlem. The one thing that bothers me with these tall buildings is they make them too tall. I fear heights.

People say I am too aggressive. Too aggressive is not waiting for them to come up with an answer but investigating the case myself and coming up with my own answer. I was raised never to take anyone's word to be God's word. So find out for yourself, and I find out by investigating things. They want you to put your brain in your pocket and to believe. Why do I have to believe anybody else than myself? And my daughter is the same way. Now they think I am hell, but you wait until they get a hold of my daughter! My daughter is four years old and she has a mind of her own. I was raised to believe that no one was better than me, but I wasn't better than anyone else either. I was raised to believe that I was equal.

I can do anything I want in New York and come out on top or on the bottom—it can break you or make you. Then you have the common sense in between, and that's it. You can tell a New Yorker from a non-New Yorker. They don't have a lot of sympathy for people, they don't give a damn. They don't have the compassion that outsiders have. Most people don't believe I am a New Yorker—compared with the people they know, I have a lot of compassion. New Yorkers are spoiled. They're taught the only way to get is to take, because no one gives you anything. You give them something, they want immediately to know what's the gimmick. They're so used to stealing, whether they're stealing time, money, or what have you.

Space means me, because that's what I need. I am a loner. I like to go when I want to go. Don't question me where I go because it's none of your business. I need my mind to be clear. I can walk down the street, and if there are many people around me I can't see them. I walk in my glory, and whoever I want to be at that moment, that's who I am.

Crossing 96th Street

Upper East Side

Diane

50, social scientist; born Richmond, Virginia; lives on East 96th Street.

I love the neighborhood. It's on the edge of what used to be Harlem. Just two blocks north from my house the train comes out of Park Avenue and the neighborhood drops down like a stone, just like that. Where we are it's still ultra-respectable, I suppose you would say, a secure, doorman-type, dull neighborhood. But just two blocks away is all the vitality of the slums. They used to be black slums, but now they're Spanish. There's almost no place in New York City where you can be more than a few blocks from a slum. I guess that's true of most big cities.

I was originally interested in the 90s because of the public tennis courts in Central Park. I'm not just a person who plays tennis. I'm a committed, dedicated, fanatic tennis player. I moved up here when I was too young and too poor to afford private clubs. Since then I've joined half a dozen tennis clubs and I still play on the public courts in the park. Mrs. Kennedy—Mrs. Onassis—also plays there on the public courts. A lot of people won't: they think they'll get mugged, walking to and from the tennis courts.

My living arrangements here will really make you laugh. In this building, which is a co-op, we own the southwest penthouse. It has an unobstructed southern view and an unobstructed view to the west overlooking Central Park, so we can see the sunset. We do a great deal of penthouse gardening, and in the summertime we live outdoors up there. But it is really too small for us to live in, so downstairs on the ninth floor, which is eight floors below our penthouse, we have a great big conventional six-room apartment. It's a very inconvenient way to live, but there are a lot of advantages. Complete privacy if you want it. I can go alone to my penthouse on the seventeenth floor and really it's better than having a room of your own. It has a kitchen, a living room, a bedroom, and this world about those spaces. We have every tree you can imagine—a pine, a spruce, a crabapple, a fig—as well as a grape arbor, lots of roses, more tomatoes than we can eat, mint, a lot of flowers, a lot of bushes. I retreat to it; my books are there, my journals are there, my professional life is there. It's kind of a little doll's house, a Petit Trianon. The apartment downstairs is very dull; conventional, elegant—satin and oriental rugs—clean. The apartment upstairs is wild and wooly and dirty and windy, and just fine. Each expresses different elements of my personality.

I'm a peculiar person from a residential point of view. I own a lot of houses. I have a house in Puerto Rico and one on Fire Island. I live in a lot of places. Even on 96th Street I live in two places. We were at Fire Island last weekend and we'll be spending the Memorial Day weekend in Puerto Rico. I've never thought of distances as a barrier—I think of time as a barrier. I love having a summer house nine floors upstairs. I don't have to get in a car and drive to be in the country. I can take the elevator, then cook out. I'm efficient in my use of time. I never have enough time, I'm always running, and that dictates the use of space, doesn't it?

The fastest way to get around Midtown is on your own two feet. When the traffic is paralyzed it's very often quicker to walk. I often walk in my own world. I'm not a very visual person, unless I make an effort to be. I tend to live inside my own head. I'm oblivious to most of what's going on around me. I don't have a seeing eye. It's very nice not to see. I never see dirt, or wrinkles, or spots, I never see unpleasant things. I'm more likely to see pleasant things. If a tree in the park has suddenly burst into bloom because it's spring, I see that, but I guess I only perceive what pleases me. I have very good censors in my eyes which block out a great deal of evil. There are too many stimuli coming at us all the time, I think, and I can't handle that much. There's so much noise, all our senses are bombarded and I cut them off like they were switches. I don't hear anything, see anything, feel anything. I just—you know—protect myself.

I would be the easiest person to mug, but I'm not a muggee. I don't walk as if I'm going to be mugged. I walk as if I own the park. I feel that way, that Central Park is mine and you're here with my permission. Nobody would dare touch me as long as I'm feeling that way.

I probably see the top of New York, I probably see only the pretty parts of it. I have little occasion to visit the unpleasant sections. I go where the tourists go—where there is no poverty, no misery, no hunger. Everybody has made an effort to make what I see pretty. And I have made an effort to make what I see pretty, to make my own house pretty.

Where I grew up in Richmond, Virginia, it was between suburban and rural. We were close to other houses except for the immediate vicinity, which was woods and fields and a stream. I had my own room. I used to think everybody grew up that way. I arrived in New York in 1954, and I think for the last twenty-odd years I have regarded myself as somebody who is just passing through New York City. If I'm in Cairo and someone asks me where I come from, I'll say "Richmond, Virginia," though in fact I haven't lived in Richmond since I went away to Vassar at seventeen. I'm in transit. I'd rather live anywhere else in the world than in New York City. That's why I'm a transient.

I firmly intend to leave New York today! I have said that for quite a few years. I hate living here. It's too crowded—too many people. I don't like that. I like the excitement but I don't want to pay the price. Though obviously I am paying the price; I am living here. But I don't really take advantage of New York. When I lived in Boston I would come down for a week and really take in all the museums, every show on Broadway. I don't any more. I'm too wrapped up in my mundane activities. I play tournament bridge and tournament tennis. I raise my own garden. I have so many ties. I'm on a lot of boards and very active in volunteer work. But these activities essentially I could carry on in Richmond. Isn't that tragic? The books I read, I could read in Richmond—I don't use the library here.

Space—infinity—I search for it. You can see how important it is to me physically. It has dictated where I live. I won't look at an apartment which doesn't have an unobstructed view. A penthouse is not enough. It has to be the highest penthouse around or it doesn't accomplish the purpose. It's not enough just to be high, because other people are high too. I look for a feeling of space all the time. One of the chief status symbols in the company I work for is a corner office, with windows on both sides. Wouldn't that be nice? So you could see, you could really see.

But I don't mind crowds because I don't suffer from claustrophobia. My husband and I spent an hour and a half stuck in the elevator. We had just been to a dance class and we practiced some of the steps we'd learned. We had a very nice time. I'm not afraid of being crushed in the subway. They push physically, to make room for just one more, like football players. I don't like it, but it doesn't bother me. I'd rather do that than waste half an hour. I don't feel all that crowded, but then look at the extremes to which I go to avoid feeling crowded. I have an extra apartment in my building so I can have a feeling of openness. That's an extreme in a city, in a high rent district. If everybody felt the way I do, the city would be in terrible trouble. I hate my beautiful ninth-floor apartment because it is so confining. I never look out there, I look in, and I don't like that. If I want to be out, I go out on the terrace.

Jeanne

actress; born Washington, D.C.; lives on East 71st Street.

I grew up a few miles outside of Washington, near the university, in a typically middle-class neighborhood. I chose to live in New York because there was theater here and I wanted to do serious theater. I didn't have the money to get established in an apartment that I would like, so it has been sublet all the way down the line. One reason why I'm taking a regular job for a while is to save enough money to move out of this place. This is the cheapest apartment in New York, so I could afford the rent when I was on the road, even though when you're on the road you usually have to pay for lodging.

Now I want to start living like a human being. First of all, there is no space; second, the light. It is very dark. You get no noise because it's way in the back, but there's no sun, no light, no space. And the next biggest thing that bothers me is the bath. The bathtub is in the kitchen. I love the bath and the water and I am always in there, making up and washing. So I want a nice big bathroom. I feel very walled off in here, very cellular, very enclosed. The nearest excuse, I find myself out the door. If I felt very comfortable in my apartment, I think I would be in more—and have my friends in more.

I like the area. I like all the East Side. It's very clean, very neat. The people seem normal. There are not these crazies running around, these addicts. Whereas over on the West Side, where a lot of actors live, in the 70s and 80s, if you go one block over to Broadway or one block over to Columbus, all of a sudden you see all kind of weird riffraff walking along. I just like to feel, you know, like I'm at home and in my own element. I enjoy walking to a clean shop and seeing nice people—or they seem to be nice.

This immediate neighborhood is very strange because right out here there are a lot of singles' bars. I had occasion to walk up the street for the first time one hot day in August. I went up First Avenue, and I thought there had been a robbery or an accident or something. The street was flooded with people, just hundreds and hundreds of people were hanging out on the street. I couldn't walk by on the sidewalk. Around this immediate area you find a lot of young single people who work in advertising agencies or in public relations or in television, that type of thing. There are millions of people in this city, and everyone is very lonely. So they go out and look for other people. But it gets into this vicious cycle where people meet and they go out for a date and that's it. And then there is somebody new, because the town is filled with millions of people, and nobody seems to stick to any one thing. They're all running around looking for something and they don't know what—all these single people looking for somebody, looking for love if you will.

The city runs you so fast. Really, it's like rats trapped in a cave sometimes. This past winter, I just stopped. I said, "What am I doing? I am always moving, always busy, where is it all going?" You don't have time to look into yourself and just make sure you're going the way you're supposed to be going, that you feel what you're all about. There's so much to do, there are so many people, so many things to happen. I like the fast pace, but you can really get run over by it all.

I was very, very career oriented and I am still, but I think I have to take care of myself or I'm going to run myself into the ground. You find you're getting hostile. I always had it fairly easy before coming to New York, and then when I came here, all of a sudden I was just another nameless face, trying to make my way. And it did become very difficult. I really began to lose my identity. So I feel that by getting back to the things that are me, and giving myself the things that I need, I will feel at home with myself, and therefore when I start auditioning heavily again, I'll project a different image.

I feel, having traveled quite a bit, that New York is really unique. The life and the energy in the city is incredible. When I come in on the train from Washington, or fly in from somewhere, as soon as I get near the city the adrenalin starts pumping. All of a sudden my heart is beating faster and I'm moving much faster. People are going places, rushing along the streets, it doesn't matter what day, what time of the year. And everything is so compact in Manhattan, you can go all around in no time at all.

I find that I'm very high-geared anyway, that's why I love New York. I love to look at the people, at the buildings, at everything. I think the tall buildings are beautiful. All along Sixth Avenue, Third Avenue—some of those buildings are really gorgeous. But there's no space in New York, no space at all. That's part of its charm, its magnetism. The interaction always on the street with the people—you have to face up to that or you'll die. And you get to cope with it all. But I think maybe that's why the apartment is so important to me at this time.

Upper East Side

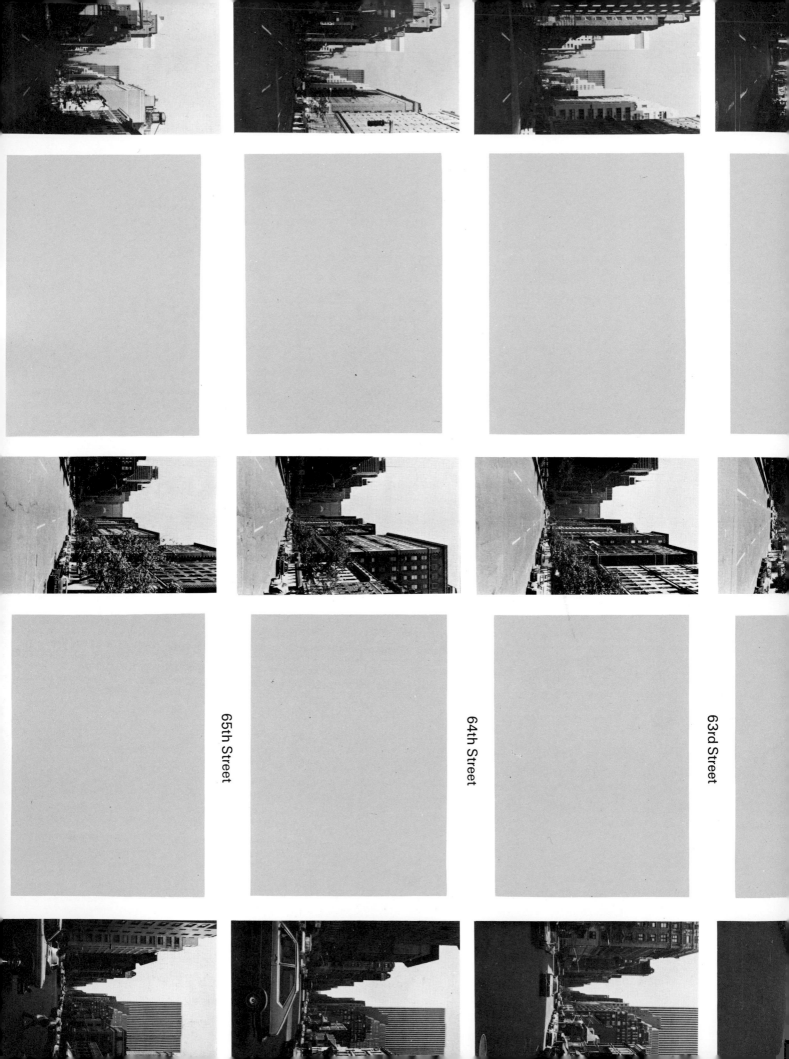

65th Street

64th Street

63rd Street

Lexington Avenue

Park Avenue

Madison Avenue

62nd Street

61st Street

60th Street

Midtown

Peter

30, film distributor; born New York City; lives Midtown.

Business—that's the only reason I live in New York. I don't like it. I don't find it at all pleasant. When I'm in town I don't have the time to go to the theater or to enjoy a lot of the things that are here. I have so much work to do. I sort of hole up here and very often I don't go out of the place. I know a lot of people who live in the city, both from business and socially, but people live in a very isolated way here I think. If you live in the country and you feel like going out, you can go to a bar and you run into a couple of friends, sit around and chatter. Here, that's not the case, unless you call some friends up and say "Let's meet." It takes a lot of arranging.

I've never really felt at home in the city. I grew up in the suburbs, in a nice sort of country area about thirty miles outside of New York. My parents have a house that Louis Tiffany built for one of his three daughters. We have a lot of property around it and we face south on Long Island Sound. A lot of trees. It's quite nice. I still go out there on weekends.

Since I got out of Harvard I've moved around a lot. I got into the film business a little over three years ago, with a partner who lives in Bermuda. The idea was that we would run the company out of Bermuda and might come to New York maybe once a month or less. Instead, we just went to the beach, went out drinking and had a good time, and no work got done. So I decided we'd have a company apartment in New York. The next thing we were producing a movie which we shot in the New York area, and I found I was living in New York. I'm traveling over half the time, because I can generate more business when I'm traveling and I can't get much work done here. So I come back here and basically catch up with the paper work and accounting and all that.

I chose this apartment because it's living space and office together, which is fairly unique in the city because we have zoning laws. By some quirk, the line between residential and commercial runs halfway through this building. So the landlord has tenants who live here and people who rent office space and also a lot of prostitutes—though he's kicking most of them out. In a perverse way I like the building, as I know the doorman and I know the owner. It's about a hundred apartments but, you know, you hear a little about this apartment, that apartment, what's going on.

The neighborhood I find very convenient for business and also for pleasure. There are a lot of good restaurants and discotheques, places to go. Times Square is a big porno area, but this little area, just a couple of blocks, is sort of another outpost of massage parlors, prostitutes, topless bars. It's a little tacky, but there are also a lot of expensive apartments with professional people.

I don't walk too much. Nothing to see. In the midtown area everything is fairly boring now, just a bunch of office buildings.

New Yorkers on the average have a much faster pace than any other people I know. You hear people just go crazy working hard. I know people in advertising who say that if you can do well here, you can go to any other city and be one of the top people for very little work. I find this in the film business—if you go to Los Angeles or Miami or Latin America, it's so much slower. The pace is almost an addiction. I don't say I like it, but it's almost like a necessary evil. It means getting five times as much business done as I would if I lived in Miami.

When I first lived in the city in '68, I enjoyed how vibrant it was. I was working in Wall Street, and working very hard, doing deals, and I sort of enjoyed that. But I spent four years living in the West Indies and then in London, in places where the pace was more civilized, and I can't tolerate it now. There are a lot of people in this city who are completely off the wall. You find a lot of business people hate New York, but they still stay here because they make a lot of money. I think that, more than anything else, New York is money. For Americans money is a game anyway. Money is sort of a way to keep score in this big game that most Americans play, the big game that is the whole of our economic system. I am an active participant in that game. I love it. It's not that I have money pouring in, because I have huge bank debts—but it's the idea of making a deal.

Most people lose in this game, most people really struggle, you know. They have a walk-up flat on the fourth floor and they have to take the subway every day. And because of that, I think, if you win on the game you find it very exhilarating, because you're competing with six million other people. It's competition, it's power. I don't know if it *is* power. I think it's striving to be truly independent, I think that's a lot of it. For me it is.

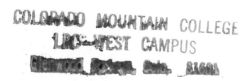

52nd Street at Park Avenue, looking west. ▷

25

52nd Street

51st Street

50th Street

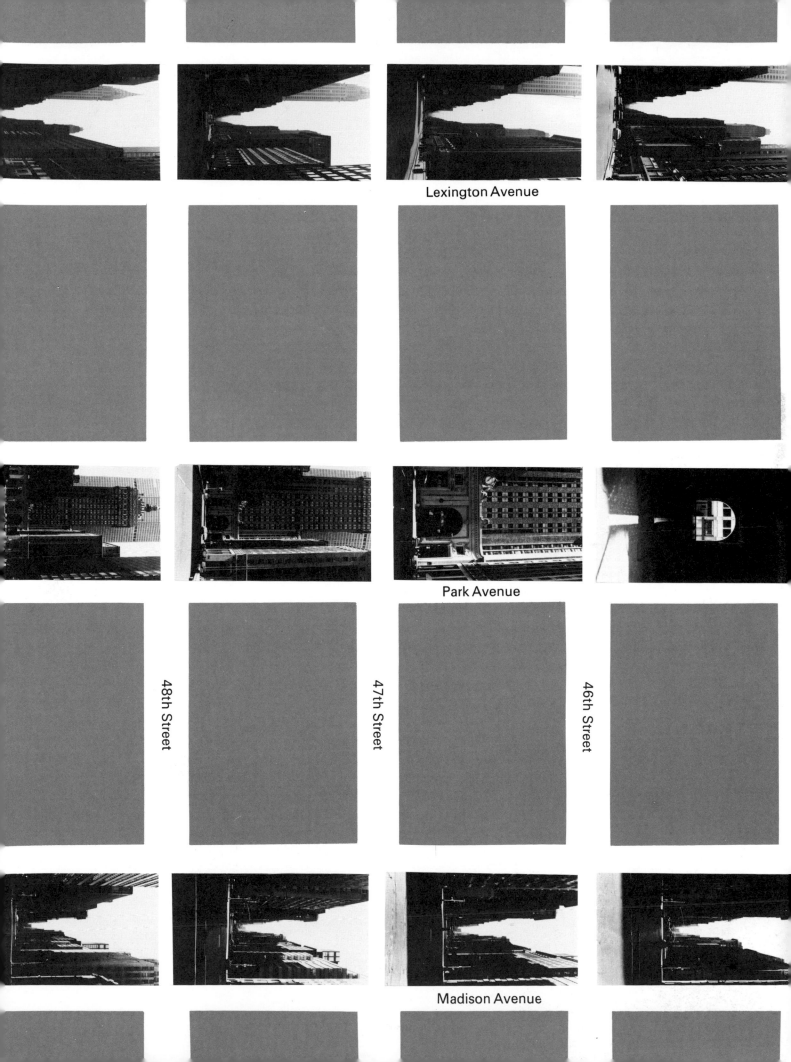

Lexington Avenue

Park Avenue

48th Street

47th Street

46th Street

Madison Avenue

360° vertical view: 41st Street, between Park and
Lexington Avenues.

Sixth Avenue (Avenue of the Americas) at 58th Street, ▷
looking south.

52nd Street

51st Street

50th Street

Madison Avenue

5th Avenue

49th Street

48th Street

47th Street

6th Avenue

47th Street

46th Street

45th Street

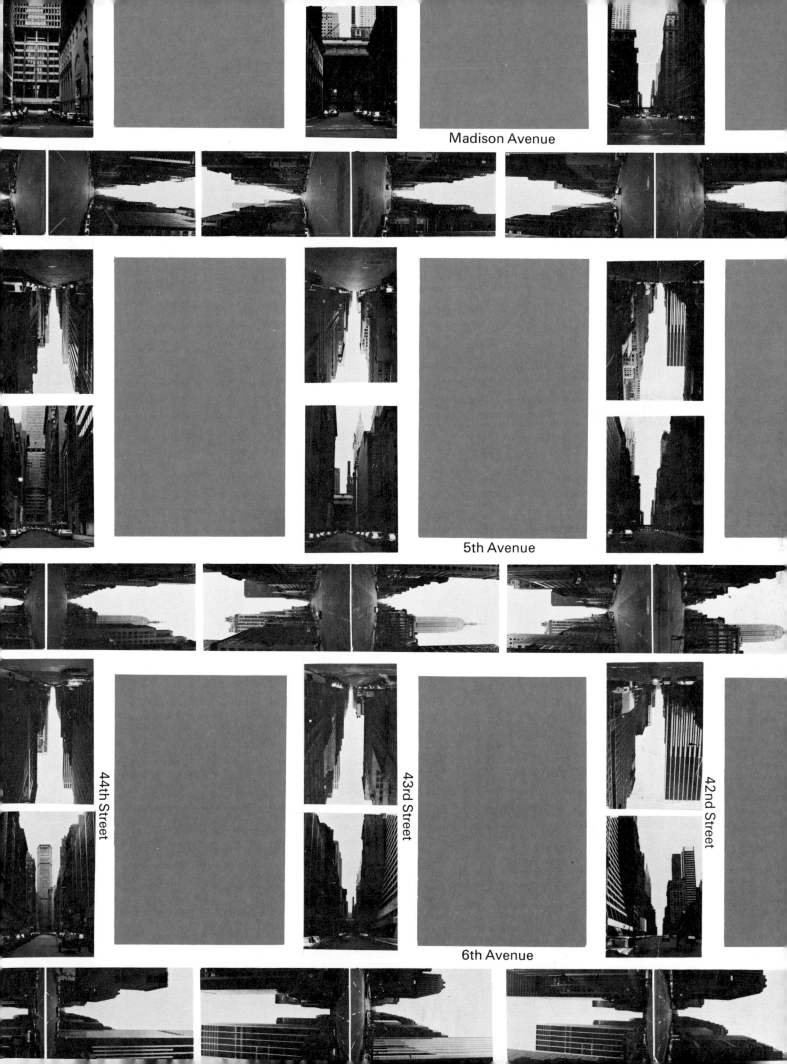

Madison Avenue

5th Avenue

44th Street

43rd Street

42nd Street

6th Avenue

Madison Avenue at 42nd Street, looking north.

Gramercy Park

Barry

32, photographer; born in Brooklyn; lives in Gramercy Park area.

I lived in Brooklyn until I was about fourteen. It was a lower-middle-income neighborhood of Jews, Italians, and—later in the Fifties—Puerto Ricans and blacks.

It was a rough place to live as a child in the Fifties—you know, gangs, rocks, leather jackets, chains, and whips. There was a lot of physical fighting. In comparison to modern war in Vietnam and stuff like that we were playing games, but it was very serious at the time for us as children, because you could get hurt easily. You had to be very careful and wear some kind of identity badge that said you were part of a gang, so if someone messed with you they had to deal with your friends later. Now I live on Third Avenue and 17th Street, near Gramercy Park. Almost all the buildings were built in the Twenties. It was a very elegant area and still is, but it has come down. I have a small apartment, just a place to sleep.

I am a photographer. I work with a group of artists in an advertising agency and photographic studio. It's on 28th Street and Park Avenue South. The real Park Avenue is in the 50s actually, which is about a mile and a half from here, and we hope to move up that way. Then we'll be in the district with the big-ten top agencies.

Of the eighteen people that work here, at least twelve of us are on the art side, so it's a creative community, a group effort as opposed to just a one-man show. They work on your ideas with you and you work on their ideas with them. You get a lot of creative feed and the melding makes your own work larger than it could be on its own.

That's what the city is all about—interaction. You probably talk to fifty people a day; even in the streets you're bombarded by people. As a photographer I'm always looking for new types. You learn all the new fashions by watching people and you get a feeling for the costumes people wear. You see, each group has its own costume. It's a motion picture, I just keep feeding it into my head. I've done it ever since I was a kid and I've trained myself to pick up information very quickly and to process it. If I really want to look closely at people on the streets I wear sunglasses, so I don't challenge them when I am really looking intensively. I like to walk. I don't stroll, I walk. I have a destination and I am healthy, I like to move quickly. I like to look like an aggressive man.

Third Avenue at 17th Street,
looking north.

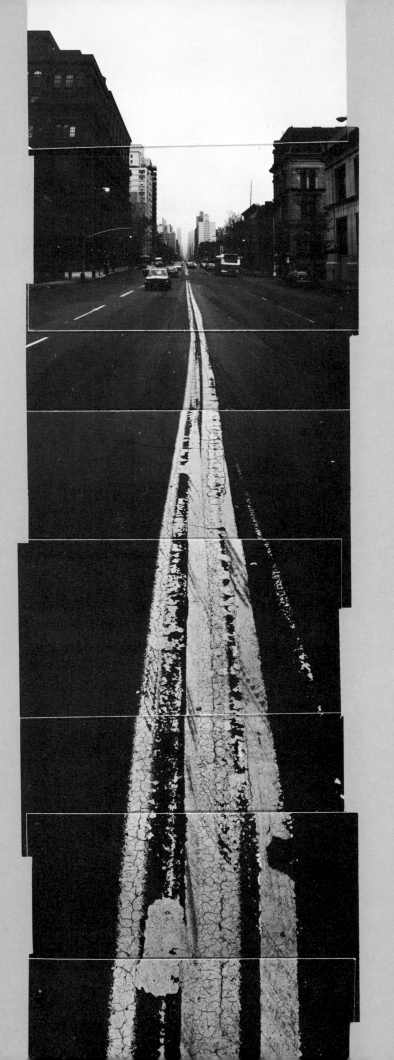

Third Avenue at Cooper Square
(East Village).

I am not fearful of the city at all. I have what I call street sense. I've lived in the East Village and in other heavy areas and I never had any problems. I haven't been mugged or robbed once since I was twelve years old. I understand the attitude that I have to project on the street to be safe. I don't want to be so tough that someone has to challenge me, but then again I don't want to look so weak that they think I am an easy victim. If you don't look like a victim, if you seem to be aware and you're moving in one direction, in a straight line, it doesn't seem to be any problem.

I really do like this place a lot, but I know many people who hate it, from outside. They can't get out of here fast enough. It's a very intimidating city. One block to the next, you're always being hit by different people. Unless you really know the city, you never feel comfortable because there are so many different experiences. You have to be ready to take the unawareness and the uncertainty and incorporate that into your pleasure.

I like the architecture. It's all on top of each other. I think the tall buildings are functional and beautiful. I am still awe-struck by them. I find it hard to believe that man built them. They look like something God made—man collectively must be a god if he can build things like that.

Twenty-four hours a day you can do something here. If you want to get something to eat at five o'clock in the morning, you can get it. If you want to see a movie at six in the morning, you can find it. The city never goes to sleep. So you can live the hours you choose to live, if you can afford it.

New Yorkers don't relax too much. Because of the activity they don't know how to sit still. I have learned, as I got older, to do that; rather than being active all the time I am trying to take two or three hours a day to get into myself, to sit and just concentrate on my own being as opposed to being part of this large thing. That's important.

Space to me as an urban being is not necessarily a physical thing. Everybody is living on top of everybody, walking around all the time. There's no space here. So it becomes something that you have to incorporate subjectively. I can have space in a crowded subway. I make it a mental process, feel it in my mind, by closing my eyes or just blanking out what's going on around me and being alone, even though I am sitting in the middle of a bunch of people.

Gramercy Park

Lower East Side

José

20, student; born Dominican Republic; lives in Lower East Side.

I was born in Santo Domingo. We got our own house. My father built it. He is a carpenter, a good one. But it wasn't too good there because, you know, it is different from New York where you can work and gain enough money for the family and everything.

We moved over here when I was about thirteen years old. We live on Clinton Street and Stanton. We got two apartments together because we are such a big family. We are about eight. All of us in the block, in the neighborhood, are Spanish—I mean Dominicans and Puerto Ricans. Our block is without any trees or nothing; only two blocks away they have trees for the new school. The streets are all cracked. The cars are making so much noise. And those buildings burning, falling down. Sometimes there is a building where they don't give you hot water, something like that; everybody moves out, and then they burn the building, that's what they do. You hear music in the streets, conga, people playing basketball, all the noise in the neighborhood. When I first came over, sometimes I was afraid of those things, but now I get used to it. I used not to go out after twelve o'clock at night. Now I can go at the time I feel like going. My mother knows where I am going, that I don't do bad things in the streets.

I never have any problem in my neighborhood, either my brothers. There are a lot of gangs here, you know. I think almost all of them are from P.R. [Puerto Rico]. A gang used to be right in front of our house and we used to see everything what they do, smoking, shooting. Sometimes they take guns and shoot in the air. I don't know why. Maybe they smoke too much and they go out of their mind and do things that they don't feel like doing. Once I can remember a man was walking on the street with a bicycle and a girl passed by and the man maybe he liked the girl, and the girl she didn't like that. She belongs to the gang and she went to get the gang. There was about twenty guys and they took the man, they beat him up with chains, everything. I don't know if they killed him, that's what I saw.

I know almost everybody around my block. They know me. I know who is the bad guy, who is the good guy. So when I see the bad guy I just keep walking straight. I make believe I don't see anymore, or I just look at something else, because if you look at them, even once, and they don't like that, they might call you something or they might beat you up. When I walk I look all over to see what's happening because I like to know what's happening in the back. Because if I see anything in the front I can stop or do something to prevent any trouble. I walk slowly and I see people walking fast and I ask myself how people feel, they're all different, everybody is doing something different. Sometimes I just think about that. Sometimes I wish I could live in Queens or somewhere like that. My brother has moved there. I am getting tired, so much noise. I'd like to change, to stay home more.

They should not have so many buildings together, right? They should have more parks, so people can walk by and have a rest, and more trees on the streets. I like uptown better than downtown. Starting from 14th Street to 96th Street or 100th, it is nice, but after about 100th you get like the Lower East Side again.

I like to live here because we are getting things from New York and the government, so I thank for that. But I wish other Spanish people would remain in their country and make their country better. But people come over here searching for money because they think that New York is the best city in the whole world. Right now I have to stay in New York until I finish school. Then I am going to work for three years or whetever I need to, and when I see that I get enough money to do something in my country, a little business or something, my plan is to go back there and help those people who need help.

Now in my country, in Bonao where I lived, there are a lot of American people. It's beautiful where they live. I am thinking in the future to make houses in that neighborhood. Where the Dominicans live it's different; they got old houses, not beautiful houses like the Americans have. My brother and me, we are always talking about that. I say, "I don't know why American people go there, there is nothing they can take or get money from." But there are a lot of mines where you get gold, petroleum, all these stuff. The Americans take them, not the Dominican people. They pay Dominicans to do the work, but they get the money.

I think of space, I think of the outside of the world. Sometimes I imagine things, like how the earth is floating in the air, right? And how it was made, and what's next to us in the air. Sometimes I look at the stars in the sky and I think how they can be so far away. I go to the roof and look from there. Sometimes I go at night by myself. I like to think, you know, sometimes be alone.

Delancey Street at Essex, looking east at the ▷
Williamsburg Bridge.

Clinton Street at Delancey, looking north *left-hand page* ▷▷
and south *right-hand page.*

Little Italy and Chinatown

360° horizontal view:
Canal Street at Chrystie.
Left to right, Confucius Plaza
(Chinatown) and the World
Trade Center in the
background, plus view of the
Lower East Side.

Marc

47, artist; born in the Bronx; lives at Mulberry Street and Canal.

When I moved here I was a painter. Then I got very interested in the theater
and films. I did one film and I never painted again. That was about seven
years ago.

   I had a lot of artist friends who were looking for a place to live and we
found this building together. So we rented it cooperatively and it was very
cheap. Most artists in New York live in this kind of building, which is
essentially a loft. It used to be a warehouse. I had to put in my own shower,
my own sink, to really build the place myself, but you can fix it up exactly
the way you really want it. I have a lot of friends that live in this area. SoHo
used to be the artist community. It was really nice five years ago, but it's

got a little too commercial since the big galleries started coming down there, and the shops and the boutiques and all the restaurants. Now the tour buses go through there.

I like this neighborhood because it's residential. It's very active, it's alive twenty-four hours a day. When we first moved here we had a lot of trouble. It's one of the oldest ethnic neighborhoods in America. This side was almost all Italian when I moved here and they were very hostile to anybody moving in who was not Italian. They thought we were hippies, communists, all those words, and they really did harass us a lot. But most of the people in the building are quite well known as artists internationally and when eventually they found that out they changed their attitude completely. They are very nice now, but on a casual, superficial level. It's like, you don't bother me and I won't bother you.

Little Italy and Chinatown

This was really a neighborhood that was going down hill, but in the ten years since I moved here it is completely changed in many ways. I don't know where it came from, but all of a sudden a lot of money came into the neighborhood. Tourists are coming here now. There was only one single bank on Canal Street, all the way up; now at least six new banks are opening around here. I was told by my landlord that this is the last area of high real-estate value in New York City. There's also a lot of manufacturing—Chinese sweatshops, a lot of sewing, a lot of clothing making.

I am one of those rare people, a native New Yorker, born and raised here. Through college I lived in the Bronx. The Bronx was very different from Manhattan. It was much more like the suburbs years ago—small family houses, sort of middle-class, Jewish, first-generation immigrants. It's totally changed now; it's a terrible ghetto, one of the worst areas in New York City. It really looks like a war area there. I moved to Manhattan simply because it was the center of the art world and I just wanted to be where everything was happening. For a film maker the energy here on a cultural level is so big—even though one thinks of Hollywood as the center for films. I am interested in a different kind of film making, sort of independent, experimental film, and New York is really the center for that. I do fiction stories, but I am trying to produce, direct, and write my own film, really as an artist making a work of art.

I like New York and I like to watch it. I like to walk around, look around—I can walk for hours. New York has some of the weirdest people in the world. Partly it's the way they look, but also I think there are probably more people in New York who would be put in a mental institution if they lived anywhere else. People who walk around and live very eccentrically, who live in a dream world. I just think they are interesting to watch. There are a lot of people in New York who make up their reality, maybe because there are so many different kinds of reality in the city. People living very privately and out in the open, I mean, living in their own heads but publicly. Besides people, I like to look at architecture. One thing about New York is that there are so many kinds of different visual things. In some ways it is the ultimate surrealist city, in terms of the strict idea of surrealism, putting—what was the phrase?—an umbrella and a sewing machine on an ironing board. That's what New York is all about. There's such a combination of things here. They are always ripping everything up and tearing it down. It's bad in a lot of ways because it means there's no cultural tradition here. But also, because there isn't any old tradition, the new tradition is constantly changing.

There are so many different cultural backgrounds that get mixed up here, and the cultures influence each other much more than in any other city. The idea of the melting-pot I think in a way really works in New York—not that all become one thing, but rather all these things add to each other. So you see people who may be raised in middle-class Jewish families imitating

Little Italy and Chinatown

52

Puerto Rican clothing styles. There was a period for a while when all the Italian kids here were dressing and looking like hippies from the Village. So there is this kind of funny mixture that goes on, even though each ethnic group likes to keep with itself.

I really like living here. But my ideal is to live in New York and go out of it for the summer. Because it's terrible in the summer—too hot, too noisy, too polluted.

Everything outside of New York looks like a small town, simply because this is so big and so heavy. I am not impressed by the big buildings because they're part of my life. I was raised with them. Maybe when the World Trade Center was built I was pretty impressed by that—I mean, it was a little frightening. When I come in from New Jersey by car, maybe that's the time I am really impressed by New York. The problem is that it's sometimes difficult to connect my sense of living here in this block, my sense of my own space and environment, with the reality of what the city looks like to someone else coming in from outside of it. New York has a strange effect on space for me. It has such straight streets that frequently you look down them and it looks very unreal. You can look from here straight down to the Empire State building and it's very flat. It all looks like a stage set, and somehow you lose a clear sense of space. I don't feel it's like thirty blocks, more than a mile; it could be two blocks away. Things seem compressed sometimes. Space becomes distorted.

If I think of space, I think of my own living space mostly. Because in some ways that's the most important thing for me, to have a certain kind of space that I can move in and feel free in and feel my mind can work in. I think of New York being vertical, and if I think of space outside of my immediate environment I think of space going up and down. Maybe my environment is horizontal and the outside is all vertical. It must be the buildings that do that and the fact that the space between two buildings is like a column of air between walls, I guess that's what makes me think vertically outside. Horizontal space is like laying it all out and organizing. And the vertical space outside is collecting a lot of visual information—people here, a billboard there, a noise here—so I am constantly jumping, up and down and all around.

Little Italy and Chinatown

360° horizontal view:
Mulberry Street at Grand
(Little Italy).

Tony

49, community leader; born and lives in Little Italy.

I am basically a writer. I write about my own people, Italian–Americans. I was one of the founders of the Off–Off Broadway theater movement way back in the 1950s. I had a café-theater back in 1952 where we just had tables and chairs—we served coffee and pastries—but the basic thing was the theater. I produced some 200 plays by new playwrights. Al Pacino, Bob De Niro, Marisa Berenson—they had their first start with me. At least some of the people I worked with had success, although myself had not. I got so involved in helping other people get their work seen that I only produced one full play and one one-act play of my own which got nice notices. Then I organized the Italian–American Repertory Company. But there was no money. I moved to six different locations, because as soon as the landlord saw that you had a crowd he would raise the rent. In 1972 I gave that up because it became too much.

Little Italy and Chinatown

I got married in 1970. Right now my wife works and I do whatever I can to earn a few dollars. I don't work at a nine-to-five job because I feel I am a creative person.

I got involved in my community. We got together and organized a group called The Little Italy Restoration Association. We had an exhaustive program to do with health, education, culture—which was my department. Then the association became very political and they fired me. I have been out of there now for a year and a half and they have not been able to raise a dollar. But as a result of that I got involved in the life style of the people of Little Italy on a very strong level. I am now this year going to run as a district leader. I am not a politician, my main concern is the people in the community. I want to get them the kind of help that I think they need and wipe away the years and years of discrimination. It's like you pick up the newspaper and some hoodlum or some crook or burglar is arrested and his name happens to be Italian, they immediately connect him with an organized crime family. They call it the mafia. I maintain that a criminal is a criminal, no matter what his race, creed, color or nationality.

**Mulberry Street at Grand, looking north (Empire State ▷
Building in the background).**

55

Little Italy is called Little Italy because when it first started being populated in the early 1900s it was in a sense a microcosm of big Italy with its separate principalities. When my family came from Sicily they went to a neighborhood where they could communicate with people, to a particular block, Mott Street, that was all Sicilian. The thirty-seven blocks of Little Italy, at the height of that immigration, were separated into little principalities. Of course, most of the blocks were basically Sicilians and Napolitans because those were the two poorest groups that came. But they all came.

I was born and grew up in Little Italy. I could at that time go from Canal Street all the way to Bleecker Street without meeting anyone but an Italian. Now Little Italy is a dying community. Not only has the housing stock deteriorated and the interiors of the buildings, but the people themselves are very nostalgic, they don't have anything to live for. They're senior citizens, most of them. The Chinese have been moving in. They own properties, they move two or three families into one apartment, in three, four small rooms. It's overcrowded. The Italians who are still here are trying desperately to hold on to a little piece of their own community.

It is a very provincial neighborhood. When I was getting jobs for young girls last summer, one of the mothers came and wanted me to get a job for her daughter. I said I had the perfect job for her, at the City Housing Authority. It's on the other side of Canal Street, she could walk there. "Oh", she said, "she has to go out of the neighborhood now? Get her a job in the neighborhood." It took me two hours to finally convince her that the best thing she could do is to give her daughter a taste of the outside. People call me the unofficial mayor of Little Italy. I am the guy that everybody comes to for advice.

Little Italy is the safest place in the world. When the Italian man marries a girl, he supports her, he doesn't want her to work, she has to stay home and take care of the babies and the house for him. After she gets through with the housework, she goes to visit some girlfriend, and they lean out the window and look up and down the street and watch everything what's happening. If they see somebody strange going into a building, they immediately call the corner store—"Hey, there's a stranger walking into number so and so. Check him out." So in a sense the women are the police force of the community.

Unfortunately I don't speak Italian. Until I was six years old I spoke fluent Italian. Then there was this attempt by the government to make people American, Uncle Sam. So my father and mother used to tell me, "No speak Italian, speak English, we are in America now." So I had a mental block against it. I think I will get hypnotized to try to break that block.

In fact I feel that the whole melting pot is wrong. You should never try to take out from a person his roots. The Italian—American needs to be able to find an identity for himself. So I try to tell my people that they are the

Little Italy and Chinatown

greatest because their blood is the blood that flowed through the veins of the greatest people of the world, the founders of the laws, the Roman Empire. And I say when they came to America they added another dimension to their personality, which makes them a more universal person.

I think the beauty of New York is its separate little communities. I would hate New York to be integrated ethnically. Every time the city has tried to build a housing project in which they are forced by law to maintain a certain ethnic balance and make it a melting pot, it doesn't work. The melting pot melts. There are internal frictions between one ethnic group and another. It is destroyed, broken up, not cared for. There is nothing in a housing project to make people happy. One building like another, like another. It makes them feel like they are in a prison. That's something I fought for—to keep speculators from coming in and buying up properties and then building high rise. I think that would destroy the character of the neighborhood.

I am not impressed by the tall buildings. The twin towers [the World Trade Center] is the only building that frightens me. I think they are very badly situated, very badly constructed, and I envision a tragedy happening some time in the future. The few times I have gone to that area there is a tremendous howling wind around there. It has been proved that the air currents have become two or three times stronger than they used to be. It's all glass and monster steel. When I see buildings like that—and they're coming up all over the city—I feel one day I'm going to go crazy and go around with a shotgun and shoot the glasses out of the windows.

Space—I am happier not in a large space. I hate country, I am a city boy. In fact I am happy in a crowded elevator. I get the same feeling in a big elevator that's empty as I get in the country. To me New York is not a big space, it's a small space, because I know every corner of it. There are certain neighborhoods that I will go to and be very cautious, but I have a psychology about how to behave in those neighborhoods. I believe that people instinctively sense your fear if you show fear and that's what makes them attack you. So when I am walking anywhere in the city, I walk proudly and with assurance and I carry myself as if I know exactly where I am going.

Mott Street at Canal, looking north *left-hand page* ▷
(Little Italy) and south *right-hand page* **(Chinatown).**

John

about 25, manager of a shop; born in Hong Kong; lives in Chinatown.

Let me start at the beginning. Right now in Chinese the direct translation of San Francisco is "the mountain of gold." For people in the old China the expression of America is that every street was paved with gold, that once you arrived in United States you would be rich. A lot of people, when they came over, they didn't know the sweatshop, they didn't know the discrimination. If they knew about it, they wouldn't come at all.

The Chinese came to San Francisco first. When they built the railroad they needed cheap labor, so they got the China man. And now that the railroad has been finished the China man has no place to go. The white man starts to be afraid because they are grabbing the white man's job. And they start to kill them. So the Chinese go to north, go to south, go to east where there is less discrimination, less conflict, you see. Then they are squeezed on to one basic job, that's the laundry. And that's the so-called lowest, lowest work. But they manage to support their families with hard work. They manage to save, work and save, until they go back to China. In the meantime they support the family that live in China. And when they were back in China they said they were making a billion, they lived like a king. But actually it was a make up story. They were working sixteen, twenty hours a day to save.

I was born in Hong Kong. I've lived in Chinatown for twelve, thirteen years. I have my business here. It is very convenient. Actually, it depends how you look at it. The young generation, they want to live outside due to the fact that they can speak the language. But the elder people, if they live out they will be very lonely because the young will be out to work, the children will be out to school. They can't speak to the neighbors. So they would more prefer to live in Chinatown. We have five senior citizen centers in which they can get together, have little games, talks, and movies, where they can spend their time happily.

Chinatown is so-called a ghetto. A ghetto is supposed to be narrow streets, no high-rise buildings, no beautiful scenery. This is a rotten spot when the Chinese first start with it. They tried to work on it and improve it. There are old rotten houses in some parts in which the bathtubs are still in the kitchen and you have to take a shower with nobody at home. Now there are some that are bought by the Chinese merchants and renovated into so-called better living conditions. And also there is a project, Confucius Plaza, up at the Bowery—750 apartments, very nice conditions. It has been 120 years that it has been so rotten, but somehow we live here happily. We live our own way, we don't bother the other side, you don't bother us, I hope. They say the tourists bring Chinatown money. Actually it is not the tourist that makes Chinatown wealthy, it is the Chinese himself. People who find jobs outside, make money, eventually they have to come back to shop and buy because this is their community, this is their food.

My cousins are American born and felt that, because they were Chinese, people call them names, laugh at them. They couldn't take it. They said, "Why am I Chinese?" But after a while they're more mature, they see through it, and they're so proud to be Chinese. They live outside, but every Sunday or every time they have a chance they always come to Chinatown. Now the Chinese mother tries to have as much time as possible with her children, teach them the language, actually force them to come to Chinatown, to Chinese school, Sunday and Saturday. So at least they can learn some Chinese language, also literature. They might forget after a while when they go to, let's say, junior high school and they have to put more time in the regular school. Maybe they forget after a year, but who care? At least they know how to speak; it would be in their mind then, you see. That's the idea.

The population in Chinatown keeps building up. There are always jobs available and it's getting more exciting, much more economic improved. But in the meantime the amount of crime has raised. In Chinatown juvenile delinquency is one of the greatest problems of today. Somehow we have to solve this problem ourselves. An outside force might not do a good job of it. There has to be a Chinese organization, with people who are reputable in charge, to start up a plan, to replan the community so that we would have no disappointment toward the tradition.

Chinatown has been expanding every week, every day, all directions. If there's any housing available they take it. A lot of Chinese merchants buy Little Italy buildings and turn them into their community. And Little Italy has been afraid. They start to reform and not to sell the buildings any more. Otherwise there is no more Little Italy. We don't want to take too big steps because if you take too big steps there is always another force that will hit you back. If you take over Little Italy, they will form a group and kill you. So little by little let them accept it.

In Chinatown the work consists always of twelve hours a day, so that you have no spare time for walking a lot. Just straight to the work and the money and straight back home. You sweat, you work for long hours and you don't spend, and later on you will be okay. That's the idea, the philosophy. Work and save and keep happy and later on you will be okay. That smile on the face, people come to you.

When we have vacations we always pick Chinatown, no matter where we go. We go to Canada and Toronto is always the first stop, because there is Chinatown there. Somehow we feel deep in ourselves that China is more kind to us. I do not mean that when we go to other places people spit at us, but deep inside we feel more at home, because of the food, because of the language.

360° horizontal view:
Chatham Square (Chinatown).

I haven't had a good chance to explore the white community, in a way. Only while I was in school, like from elementary to college. But that's a different atmosphere. When you're in school, no matter what your race is you ought to talk to each other. There is not so much so-called discrimination. But when you're out in a job, in the real community, then it's a different world, am I right? When you are challenging one the other, then you feel it happening. Because I work in the Chinese community there is no such thing, but from what I heard there can only be a limited point of success in the American community.

There is not so much discrimination as toward the blacks and the Puerto Ricans, but the Chinese never speak up. We always do our own things and take whatever comes to us; any force has come to us, we just take it. If you turn and fight back, you will have a bad image and later on the young ones

Little Italy and Chinatown

will have another force coming at them. I mean, if the first generation take it, slowly, slowly it will disappear. Gradually the whites look at Chinese differently. They are nice, although they look like a weak pie, but they are nice. The young ones are now free of so much hatred and discrimination. They will be living more happily. Now the blacks can't take it any more— they fight back, fight back. Ten thousand years later, there will be another discrimination.

Space means money in Chinatown, a lot of money. Chinatown space almost can compare with Fifth Avenue. It is very, very valuable land. The owners are 100 percent Chinese—there are no more American landlords. This is the most expensive ghetto in the world. If the space makes money, good—right?

Little Italy and Chinatown

Wall Street Area

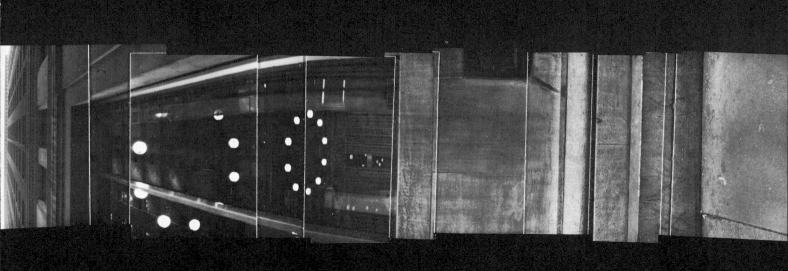

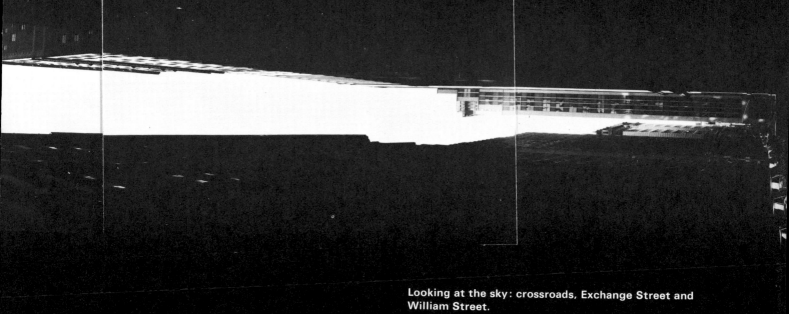

Looking at the sky: crossroads, Exchange Street and
William Street.

360° vertical view of the World Trade Center towers.

180° horizontal view from the West Side Highway at
Chambers Street exit, looking west at the Hudson River.

Tribeca and SoHo

180° horizontal view from the West Side Highway at Chambers Street exit, looking east.

Laurie

31, musician; born Chicago; lives in Tribeca.

I wanted a space that was large enough so that I could give small concerts here. I write music and also do some visual art. Most of my work is technologically oriented and I use computer electronics a lot in my music. I like to have a great deal of time to myself, just to be by myself and also to work and do whatever I want without being bothered by anyone.

Tribeca and SoHo

One of the reasons I like this part of town is that we are near the river. There is a large area of land where you can walk for a couple of miles down by the river and virtually not see anything but sand and water and be at a certain distance from the buildings, which is just marvelous. This is still a large area for importing and distributing food, so there are trucks coming in starting at five, six o'clock in the morning, but by now [mid-afternoon] most of the activity has ceased. Spaces like this are often empty for living because the smaller industries have been put out of business by the larger corporations. It's sort of like SoHo was ten years ago. After five o'clock in the

Tribeca and SoHo

360° horizontal view: West Broadway at Worth Street from the southeast corner (Tribeca).

afternoon the whole area becomes extremely quiet and there are only a few people around and you all know each other. It has a real sense of an artistic community.

I grew up mostly in a very large house near Lake Michigan, which is more like an ocean, and I never really got used to the feeling of being enclosed in a small apartment. You're always aware that six feet away there's another person on the other side of the wall. The physical environment of New York I very much dislike, but the range of people you meet and the cultural activities are something you couldn't find anywhere else—the kind of exchange with people that can happen, the way your own mind changes and you become interested in new things. For me, my mind and my work are the most important things.

I don't like the noise level in the streets of most cities. I find if it is quiet, somehow things don't seem quite as large as they do when it's noisy. Noise is the one thing which really bothers me. There are many very violent sounds and there is a tremendous amount of tension in the city. Sudden sounds raise your adrenalin level. Most of the time nothing will actually touch you,

Tribeca and SoHo

but all your system is on guard against it. You can't close your ears, you can't get away from the sounds.

I am more comfortable indoors in the city. Usually I am in a hurry to get back home when I am out. If I walk slowly and really look at things, often people speak to me and break my concentration. There is a terrible tendency for people to isolate themselves in New York. There are just so many people who come from somewhere else and who find the city very hostile; they need something secure to hold on to. Their living space is almost like a fortress and a protection.

I think of space in terms of time, when you have space between your activities, when you have a chance to somehow synthesize all the impressions that have hit you. In a city you're taking in so much information, just visually walking down a street, you become overloaded, you have to lose some sensitivity. If you have more space, more time, more relaxation, you can maintain a much higher level of sensitivity. And also, space is to me just what is in my own mind, where I can relax and really look inward into myself, without being on guard against my surroundings.

Tribeca and SoHo

View of the sky at Mercer Street (SoHo).

Steve

35, attorney; born in Massachusetts; lives in SoHo.

I grew up in Rhode Island, in a lower-middle-class family in an Italian, Irish, Catholic neighborhood. I was one of the only Jews on the block. I was a street kid primarily. I think most New Yorkers believe that once you leave New York you aren't going anywhere. To some extent that's true, though obviously it isn't really. I mean, this is a beautiful country. I've lived in several other cities and I was regarded as a freak because I had a beard, my hair at the time was longer, and people weren't quite sure what I did for a living. But here I am sure I am considered quite normal. I am an upstanding citizen, I work with a foundation, I am an art dealer. I mean, morals are different. I think this is the only place I can survive in this country. The kind of behavior that is tolerated here is much wider in scope and activity than would be tolerated in any other city in this country, perhaps with the exception of Los Angeles. People will let you do what you want to do here. The great crush of population is exactly the thing that makes it a freer place to be. Some of it is "I don't want to be involved," and I think part of it is fear, particularly of crime. But also part of it is respect for what other people are doing. I leave you alone, you leave me alone. The fact that there are only one or two murders a day in New York City is astonishing with the population that we have, and the density and closeness of people. There are more crimes in Phoenix, Arizona, than there are in New York per capita.

To be able to come in from the crush of the streets into this space and have it as empty or as full as I want is a luxury in this city. I have known people who lived in SoHo for ten years, so I have been exposed to living in a loft—however, everybody does something different with it. To live in a space like this involves expanding your own limits, not only your own physical limits, but your limits of perception. Because we are used to living in space that's defined for us and is primarily uniform, and we're used to walking through maze-like situations, from room to room. I feel this space gives me a lot of psychological freedom. This area has had for some time the tradition of being the artistic center of New York. As far as I am concerned the danger with SoHo is that the same thing will happen here as is happening to Greenwich Village. However, in saying that I also recognize that I am part of the process.

Things that go on in the streets here are astounding. You can see bankers, businessmen, prostitutes, Chinese, Japanese, Indians, blacks, people from the islands. You can see very crazy people walking around, I mean obviously crazy. And to walk through Central Park on a Sunday is incredible. On the horse track you can see the blue-blood East Side type and next to them on the grass a bunch of kids from the barrio. The park is a great social leveler because everybody uses it. To be able to view that is fantastic—the concentration of culture, energy, and people.

I walk a lot in New York. I think it's fun. I usually walk quickly because that happens to be my natural pace and rhythm. I have lived in cities all my life and nothing ever happened to me—I have never been mugged, never been held up, never been hit. Now I suspect that has to do with the attitude that I sometimes have when I'm walking in city streets, which is not always very friendly—an attitude of self-assurance, that I know what I'm doing and can take care of myself. That's part of urban survival, unfortunately. I'm usually aware of everything that goes on around me. I try to be, that's partly the way I am, and I use a lot of those techniques in my work. I think it is important to know where you are situated on a street or in a room in relation to other people. I think that kind of socialgram and placement of people is very important because you learn about yourself and other people, the points of power.

The World Trade Center is an overpowering presence in Lower Manhattan. I think it is totally inhuman in its scale. It scares me. None of the windows can be opened, the building has its own self-contained environment. It is a living being almost. The only building that really impresses me is the Chrysler Building. It was probably the last example of craftsmanship in this city and the building itself reflects that.

Mostly what space means to me is the ability to stretch out, and for me it's a totality: it's physical, emotional, psychological. And while I don't always do that, I have the opportunity, and that's part of what living in New York can do for you. Because most of what people want is here. I am talking about professions and in terms of people's goals and aspirations for themselves. I think that's why I am here. But I may be here because I am a total romantic and believe in the cultural romanticism of New York City, the big apple. It's a magic kind of place, and maybe if you stay here long enough you will be magic too.

On West Broadway, looking at the World Trade ▷
Center towers (SoHo).

On Mercer Street, looking at the Chrysler Building (SoHo).

Greenwich Village

John

32, TV director; born Boston, raised in New York City; lives in Greenwich Village.

I lived at 71st Street and Fifth Avenue for most of my childhood. It was fine. I had a nanny and we had a cook and a maid and a chauffeur. I lived there till I was sixteen and then my parents and I had a parting of the ways and I left home. It wasn't certainly a rejection of my situation. I just didn't like my parents very much and they didn't like me very much. So I left.

When you're sixteen years old it is very hard to check into a hotel, and when you walk out of your home the first thing you think about is, where am I going to eat, where am I going to shit, where am I going to sleep, and where am I going to take a shower. Grand Central Station was the place. It was an easy place to live, back then. I knew it because, when I was a little boy, my father used to make business trips from Grand Central Station and I used to go down there with my mother to see him off on the train. I was always intrigued with Grand Central Station. It seemed like a wonderful place and I think I felt very strongly about it. I stayed there about two and a half months.

I have traveled quite a bit and I can't think of any other place on the face of the earth where I can have more things at my command than in Greenwich Village. That's really why I live here. I can do whatever the hell I want whenever I want and there is no social pressure to stop me or to encourage me. I can be as active as I want or as passive as I want. I can go to bed for a year. You can't do that uptown.

I don't mean to sound fanatical but I really love my work. I try to live my work, I try to think about it most of the time. So when I walk I tend to look at things very carefully and I try to file them in my mind some place, thinking that some time maybe I'll use something, maybe just a little detail of how something looks. I am a very boring person to walk around with because I become intrigued with very boring things. But I have a specific purpose in what I'm doing. I look at silly things—fire hydrants, plaques on buildings. I try to look at everything. You know, so many people don't see things. It is astonishing to me. You're only on earth once, so you really ought to take a look at what the hell is going on around you. You ought to look at people, how their bodies move and what they wear. You should look at the physical things because they reflect the people. There is an intention for everything that's there. So you stand there and you look at it and you

decide what was the intention. Sometimes it takes more than one look and you have to think about it.

When you walk along the streets in New York you see everything at the street level; then you look up and there will be like a dress shop on the first floor, and you look up and there is a clock store and on the third floor a beauty parlor. And you just keep looking up and looking up—it's like forty cities piled on top of each other.

I love the tall buildings. The World Trade Center is ugly; there's nothing to that building, no perspective. Who the hell cares how tall it is? But the Empire State Building, it's a needle. It was intentionally built to look higher than it was, you know. It's a cathedral, the gothic architectural idea, a needle that scrapes the sky. And the Chrysler Building, with those incredible gargoyles. That's part of the power of New York, its size. If you fly over the city and you see that, you've got to know there is no place else. That's a very chauvinistic thing to say, but God dammit, there is just no place else. And to be part of that is the excitement of living in New York. You can never be a big shot in this town, because there is always something bigger than you are. But you can be part of it, and that's good enough. I love it. And there's not just one of those buildings, there are hundreds of them. And they are enormous, they are huge. The power that's involved in all that, it's incredible. And here I am in the midst of that power, and I am not getting killed, and I seem to be happy here. It's like sitting on the right hand of God. It is like you are this little tiny angel and he could clasp his hands and that would be the end of you. But he never clasps his hands on me—here I am. This town is like a big woman, like a mistress. It is unbelievable, it is terrible. But it can be a real bitch, boy, if you're depressed.

It's odd for me to find an inanimate object more powerful than I am, you know. It's like being next to a mountain or something. It is just so much larger than you are. If you fly over it, then you can be superior to it. But when you're standing at the base of it and you're six feet tall and that thing is going for ever and you know that there are ten thousand people in that building, you get knocked down by that. And I am one of them. Special club. That's why people hate us, because we are part of that power inherently. They are intimidated by the power of the town, so they are intimidated by the people who live there.

This town has a romance and a strength and a drama to it that you just can't find any place else. It's a giant theater and has the best players in the world. New Yorkers are the fastest talking people on the face of the earth. They are also the funniest people and the most generous people. It's funny you know, this town is very cynical. It's hard to cheat the average person on the street, or to cheat the town in general. It's tough to beg money if you look like a bum, because in this town there is always work, so they don't have much tolerance for bums. But if you look like a human being, if you

Greenwich Village

wear the right uniform and you speak the right language, you can walk up
to a perfect stranger and say, "Look, I'm in a jam, I need sixty cents for a
token to go home," and the guy will give you a dollar. But it's not a town
for old people, unless you have money. That's maybe a problem for everybody here: you have to have money.

Space is freedom. Power and freedom. Your own space is your own and
you govern it. When I visit the artistic community in SoHo I find most of the
space is very boring to me. There's nothing going on there. It's like abandoned
space. There is usually a large oak table in the middle of the kitchen area
and everybody sort of assembles around and the rest is left open. I would
rather fill it up with stereo and television and motorcycles and God knows
what. Do something with all this space—build a boat in it, build an airplane
in it. But they don't. What they do, they get back around that kitchen table
and they look out at all that space like there's a show going on there. But
there's nothing going on; it's all empty. They're rejecting the power that's
available to them.

I've stood on the edge of the Mojave desert in the Southwest, and in
Grand Canyon, and I haven't felt they were as big as New York. I know they
are, logically, I know they're bigger. But I don't get that sense.

Sullivan Street, looking north. ▷

95

180° horizontal view: Sullivan Street, looking west.

Greenwich Village

Sullivan Street, looking south. ▷

180° horizontal view: Sullivan Street, looking east.

Greenwich Village

Rebecca

34, photographer and audio-video technician; born Puerto Rico; lives in Greenwich Village.

My job title is videotechnician. Mainly what I do is produce educational aids for students. The job is a lot of different types of work, which I like—because if I were just a photographer, in business for myself, I would have to specialize in a particular field, like taking pictures of food, which can be very boring. And I am not a competitive person.

I came to New York City when I was about three years old and we lived in Brooklyn when I was a child. We were constantly moving for one reason or another, I think basically because my parents were trying to get us into a better neighborhood each time. Being Puerto Ricans, we always got in at the beginning and in a couple of years the neighborhood was a slum area again. So we got out. Then I left home when I was fifteen or sixteen. One of the reasons was I couldn't take moving around so much. I would just make friends and get accustomed to my school, the people, whatever, and then we would pick up and move again. So I got really turned off and I said, "I am not moving any more," and I split from home.

I won't live anywhere else in Manhattan but the Village, because the Village has a sense of community to it and, number two, because I am gay. In the beginning that played a big part in it; as an adult I really don't care too much. But also it's pretty, there are trees, the buildings aren't as tall, you don't have a big avenue running by you with all the noise and the traffic. Other than the tourists, this is the perfect place to live. And, I don't know, I like the people here much better than I like the people elsewhere. Also there is everything down here. There's a joke that most people who live in the Village, they never go above 14th Street.

When I was a kid and I first came to the Village there was an entirely different group of people. First of all the rents were not that expensive, there were not all these new high rise buildings but a lot of small brownstones. The kind of people that lived down here were artists, really, and musicians— in those days they were called beatniks. And then the place started getting more and more expensive. They started to renovate, knocking down the houses, putting up the skyscrapers. Anybody who had the money found it a desirable place to live. I don't like the skyscrapers. Number one, they block the view of the sky; number two, you can house twenty times more people in them and I don't like crowds. It's just allowing more people to be congested in a small area.

There's very little sky to see in New York, and what you can see of it most of the time it's just a lot of pollution. And the other thing you notice is that when you are in the city the sky seems so far away. It could be the atmosphere and all the junk that's in it, and also I guess visually the fact that the buildings are so tall makes the sky seem very, very far away. Recently I was in Puerto Rico; that sky is very close to you. It's strange, like you feel you can just reach out your hand and pick out a cloud. It's that close. The stars are close when you are by the ocean also. That's interesting, psychologically—I don't think it is all visual.

I always walked a lot ever since I was a kid. I don't think I walk that fast. I can't allow myself to do that because that's what everybody does here. They run around like a bunch of maniacs and that agitates me just to watch them and I don't want to be the same way.

I don't like New York, but I haven't left. I think that most people who love New York are not from New York at all, they have come here as adults. Most people who grew up in New York don't love it, they're just so used to it, they can't get away from it, and I think that's my problem too. But the most important thing—and I would be a damned liar if I didn't say it—is that being a homosexual this is the easiest place for me to be. I tried living in Vermont and I found myself coming back. I think I managed to do it for about six, seven months and then I couldn't take it. I never felt healthier in my entire life than when I was in Vermont. I was doing very healthy constructive things, and I was a lot of time by myself also, which gave me a lot of time to think and to feel like a part of the earth, like I belonged there. I don't think that living in the city I ever felt that I belonged to anything other than my apartment. I still think I am not going to spend the rest of my life here. I mean, this is not a home, this is just a room that I am renting. When you live in a city you're a transient, you're nobody, you are not in touch with nature. It's a whole different way of living. In Vermont I felt a part of the country, a human being, believe it or not. In the scheme of things you are nobody, but in the scheme of things you are also everybody. It's corny but it is like a universal identity.

I came back for two reasons. Number one, Vermont is very cold. When it's 30 below zero it does something to you psychologically. You wake up every morning and there is snow as far as you can see. It was that white, seeing that white constantly and just hearing the goddam wind blowing all the time. You have to have a lot of inner resources, you have to be very busy, and preferably with someone that you love very much, because it is really hard. But also most of my friends were in New York. And though I was busy and doing constructive things, after a while I needed the excitement which I am accustomed to. You don't get that excitement anywhere else. I know I can be distracted very easily here. There are millions of things to do in the city, run around and get stoned, party, you know, anything. You can just get lost, even watching a stupid TV set. You don't even have enough time to get into your own things, which is bad too, but it's a pace you become accustomed to. It's a habit that's very hard to break.

Greenwich Village

**360° horizontal view:
Washington Square.**

I think you have more or less the same kind of mentality on the East Coast and on the West Coast, and everything in between is a whole different world. The way people think, the way they relate, their politics, their religion, everything is entirely different. Californians are a lot more mellow, they're a lot friendlier. They have space, they don't have these buildings that we have here. And also they have the sun all the time, they're outdoors partying all the time. You can't do that too easily here. New Yorkers don't spend time in parks or sitting out in front of their buildings. New Yorkers are friendly too. I think once they realize that you're not a threat, they're almost happy to be able to talk to somebody on the street. But they are paranoid. So many millions of people here—you know, you are anonymous. New Yorkers are really okay, they're just paranoid.

Greenwich Village

Space, the Arizona mountains, yes, absolutely. You can stand on a mountain over there and you can see for ever, you can see desert, and more mountains, and cliffs. Your view is not obstructed by anything. That to me is space. Texas is space. Even if I had the largest apartment in New York, it wouldn't be enough space because I know what's outside my door. Space is anything devoid of a lot of things that obstruct the view. And definitely silence—that's very important to me. When I go out of New York City, I can't wait for you to turn the engine off, because it is death silence. And that is tranquilizing.

Greenwich Village

Chelsea

Barbara

28, secretary; raised in Brooklyn; lives in Chelsea.

I live in Chelsea, that's from 14th Street to 23rd Street. It's a relatively old neighborhood. It has mixed ethnic groups, like Italians, Spanish, Greeks, and then it has the young hip-type person. It's right above Greenwich Village and a lot of gay men live in the neighborhood too. I like my apartment here because I have a view without any other buildings. The apartment I had before was lower, you couldn't see the sunlight, and it was important for me to see the light, you know, and have the sky. What I like best is the way I can see the sky change from day to night and as it gets dark, the sunset.

I grew up in a neighborhood called Brighton Beach which is near Coney Island amusement park. It was kind of lower middle class, mainly Jewish people—a lot of old people, and a lot of young kids.

I am a secretary. When I first started in this job it was exciting because I organized the office. Now it's really much more routine and I find it kind of boring. I know I have to change. There are no windows in my office—it's terrible. It bothers me a lot. There is one building, the New York Telephone, no windows in the whole building. And then there is another, on Chase Manhattan Plaza, where the windows come out: the wind is so strong and it's so high up, the windows pop. I used to work down by Wall Street, one of the oldest parts of Manhattan. The streets are very narrow and you are surrounded by big tremendous walls. I didn't like the feeling of those buildings. They were just so big and closing in on you. And the people down there, especially on a rainy day, they all wear black. They have black limousines, they wear black overcoats, black umbrellas.

In New York City you can really stop being physically active if you don't pay attention to it. I didn't have that much money this past year, so I walked a lot. It's nice, very nice, and I can get around just as quickly. Some days I look very far ahead and around, some days I don't. I guess I'm like anybody else and sometimes I get into my own head, but I don't do that often in the city unless I am with somebody, because I always try to be aware of my safety. I guess usually I look at people like myself, the same kind of age, you know, lovers. And store windows—I look at a lot of clothes. What else? I see the niceness of the sky. I always look at the sky. I like to be reminded that there is nature around all the buildings and the people and the uptight things that happen, that there is also the sky. I don't think New York City has too much nature, other than human nature, but I see the sky that covers everybody like this common denominator—because there are so many different people, different crazies.

I think the buildings are beautiful. The skyline of New York City, it's a beautiful piece of sculpture. It's just unfortunate it's so badly polluted. But looking at it from a creative eye, lines and shapes, I think it is beautiful. I like to be in it, but not all the time—you know why? There are not enough curves. Nature always has curves, it's not only right angles. New York City, it's mostly right angles or angles. So I prefer the curves sometimes. Last summer I went to Fire Island. I spent the whole month at the beach. There are no buildings, just little houses and the beach. That was beautiful; and there were a lot of city people, so it was the best of both worlds, kind of.

When I was married, my husband hated New York City. He hated the buildings and the dirt and this and that. But my feeling is, if I am living here, there might be things I don't like about it, but I am going to make the best of it, and there are a lot of things I do like. I think it is really the best city because there is so much here, you know, so much excitement. And you can learn from it. I feel what I have learned from New York City I could never learn it anywhere else—you meet so many different people that you have to get to know. The only other big city that I really spent any time in was San Francisco. I thought it was very quiet, very relaxed. I got in my car to go downtown at 5 o'clock to see what the rush hour was like, and I couldn't really find it.

I have not traveled all that much. I did notice when I traveled, though, that the people weren't like the people I know. In New York everybody has a different attitude depending on what they are in. They are more easily recognizable because they have attitudes, whether they have a hip attitude, or a gay attitude, or a straight attitude, or a freaky attitude, you know. In other places they're just people and look who they are.

Space means the ability to be where you want to be and who you want to be. That's something I learned, because in New York City, if you don't know that . . . I mean, it was very tough for me before I learned that: that I have the peace inside myself, that I can give myself the space, say, to be quiet. You need to know that, that the only person who can give you space is you, in your mind.

Chelsea

Barbara's apartment, window towards west.

Subway at 23rd Street.

Chelsea

110

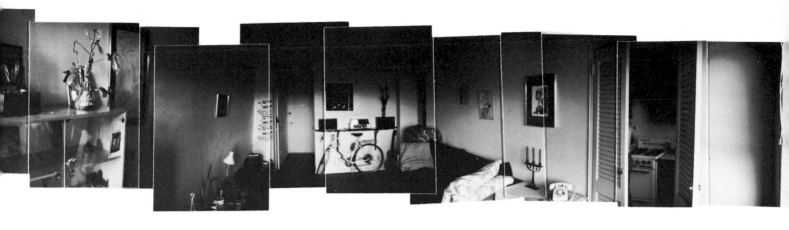

Chelsea

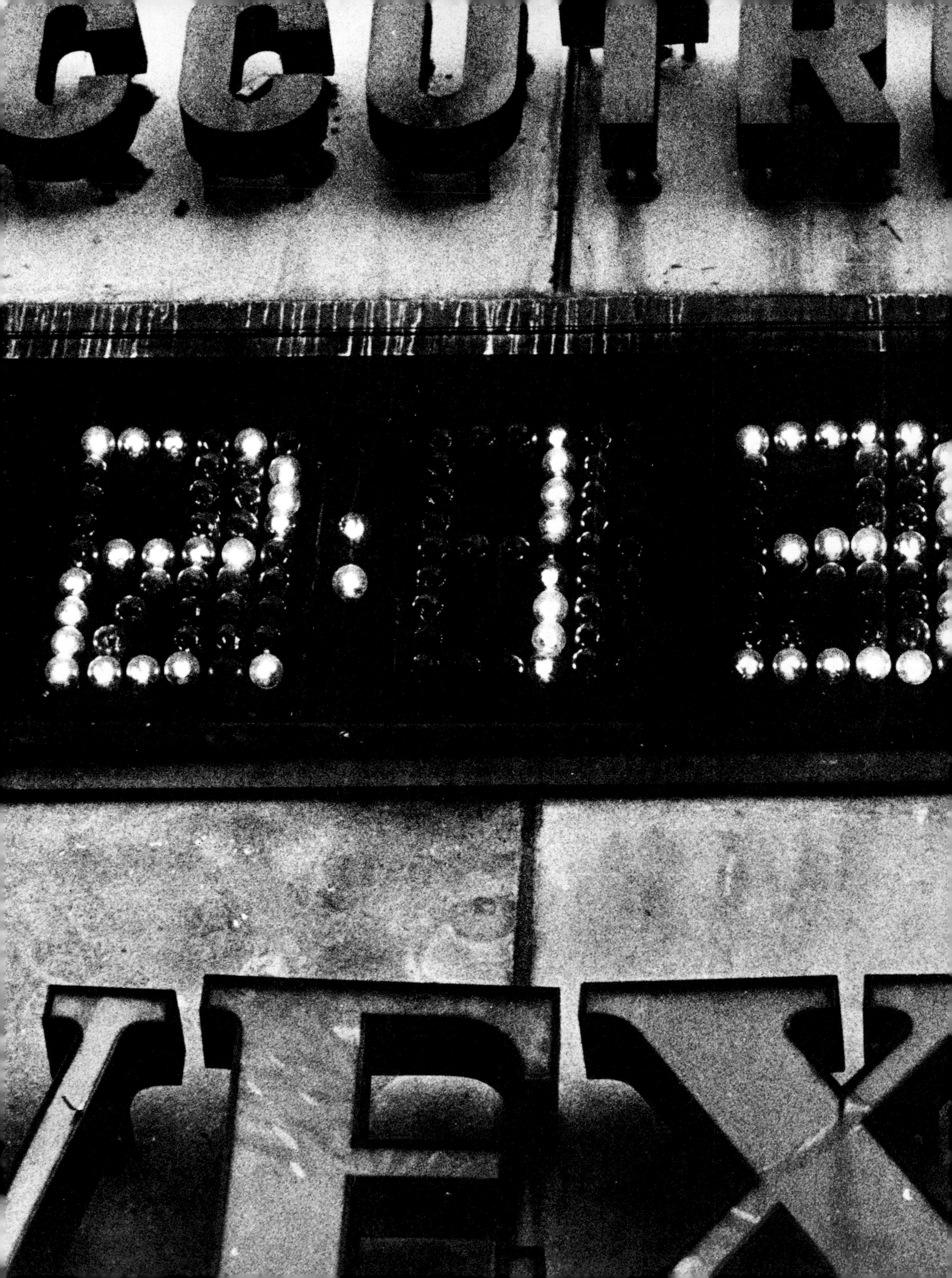

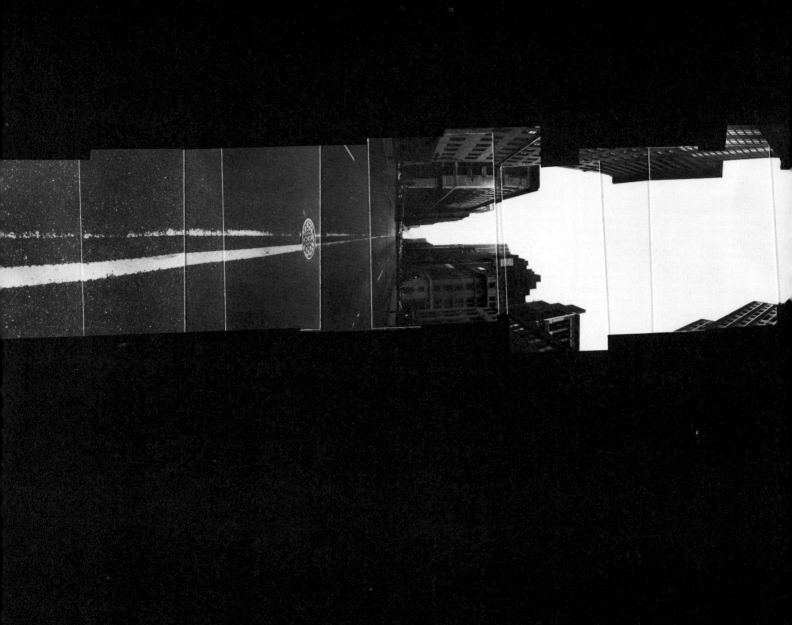

360° vertical view: Empire State Building at 34th Street.

Hell's Kitchen

Ralph

49, cook; born in Harlem; lives in Hell's Kitchen (West 40s).

The only think I like about the city is that jobs are plentiful. You have more restaurants here than you could imagine, and me being a cook, I can find a job easily because I am a fairly good cook.

This neighborhood is not bad, really. I lived in worse. In any neighborhood in New York City you just got to watch yourself. I usually walk in the streets with my hands in my pockets because if you have your hands in your pockets, nobody knows what you have in there. This I learned in Harlem. They never know if you're carrying a knife or not. People that mug and commit crimes, they'll think twice.

The high school I went to, on 116th Street, at that time was the worst in New York City. There were fights every day outside the school. You would have a little problem in school and when you got out somebody was waiting for you. Sometimes you had three or four fights going on at the same time. Harlem was bad, very bad. After school we used to play in a little park, Morningside Park, but as soon as dusk came, no matter what you were playing, you went home. It was not safe in the park. My father was very strict, we had to be home at a certain time. We were ten of us. So when my mother cooked, everybody had to be sitting at the table, everybody had to eat at the same time. If you came late, you didn't eat. I had a very strict upbringing and it helped. I am very grateful for my parents, the way they were. It kept us on the straight path. My parents came to United States from Puerto Rico. All my brothers and sisters except for my elder sister were born here. People around my neighborhood where I lived, they didn't bother me, even two or three blocks distance. They knew you lived there. It was just outside my neighborhood—they were the ones that bothered me. I guess in other cities it's that way. You are more at ease in your own neighborhood. I don't venture there any more, I stay away from neighborhoods like that.

We moved out of Harlem and went to live at Columbus and 100th, which was a fairly good neighborhood when we moved in but eventually it got bad. It just started, like an apple, to get rotten all of a sudden. We moved again, and I lived in Queens for a while. Then I settled on 43rd Street, between Eighth Avenue and Ninth. Right across from where I lived was a church, so it was fairly quiet. But outside of that lot, forget it—it was bad.

It's a good thing we took this apartment: the other, the old one, burned down right after we moved out. I can walk to work, but I would never walk

116

at night. I usually take a taxi back. At night, let's face it, at one o'clock in the morning, to walk in New York by yourself, it's not safe. But I am accustomed to it here, you know. It doesn't bother me much, except at night, because I am really a homebody. I come home, I go upstairs, and I read. I am very much interested in the psychic, telepathy. And I read cards, Tarot cards. It's a fascinating field really. You go over there on Eighth Avenue and you see a lot of Tarot readings, but they're gypsies, they'll rip you off. They work on your superstition, and this I don't believe in. Everybody is psychic, everyone, it's just some are more developed than others. That's all there is to it. When I come home from work, I usually pick up a little book and I start reading and usually it's on those subjects. If you really get involved, it's fascinating. My wife laughs at me.

You might term this a form of escapism, where I bury myself with these books—and why not? But I don't think so, because I have other forms of escapism, like painting. I paint when I have the time. I don't have much time because I have two jobs. I like anything that has beauty in it, you know. I am not what you would say a good artist, I am just an amateur, but I like beautiful things. So once in a while I look up at the sky. It's beautiful really, the clouds, the formation of clouds, the contrast against the blue sky and the buildings. A lot of people I know never look up, maybe because the tall buildings bar their way, I don't know. I am not impressed by the tall buildings. They are there, something you take for granted. If you grow up in a forest, trees mean nothing to you. You see them every day, you are not impressed. The only thing that impresses me is the art on the buildings, the sculpture. Some man created that, you know. People just don't look. In fact, one time I was picked up by Immigration, believe it or not, because I was looking up at the design on a building like a greenhorn, you know, and they thought I was a foreigner, so they asked for identification and where I was from. I am a native New Yorker.

I feel very free in New York City, although it might not appear so and to you it might seem a contradiction. But I feel very free. I can go anywhere I want, right here, from here.

Space—infinity. If you read on keen subjects like I have been reading, there is no time. Man makes time.

47th Street at Ninth Avenue, looking west. ▷

Ninth Avenue at 48th Street, looking south *left-hand* ▷ ▷
page and north *right-hand page.*

49th Street at Ninth Avenue and 54th Street at ▷ ▷ ▷
Ninth Avenue, looking east.

Upper West Side

**360° horizontal view:
Central Park, buildings to
south and west, trees and
bushes to north and east.**

Edmund

37, writer; born Ohio, lives on West 86th Street.

Probably my most formative years were spent in Evanston, which is a large
suburb outside of Chicago that really has a good racial balance. It's upper
middle class, very respectable, a rather admirable community in some ways,
but it's a little bit dull.

   I was living alone in Greenwich Village and then I got a roommate and we
heard about this big apartment. It's seven rooms and it only cost $400, so we
moved up here. I don't like the West Side too much. I am homosexual and
the Village certainly must be the largest gay community in the world, the
most open and the most free. But to get an apartment like this down there
will cost $1000.

This is a very mixed neighborhood, very strange. For instance, here on 86th Street there are a lot of older Jewish people in their seventies or so, most of them Austrian. And then one block up is mainly blacks and Puerto Ricans, and one block down is like young married people who have bought houses and fixed them up, sort of respectable middle-class types. And this particular building is very gay.

Ever since I was a little boy I always thought New York was like the center of the world and that I was on the periphery some place. It was like being invisible, which actually made me almost physically uncomfortable, that feeling of living this absolutely unnoticed life. I remember as a boy being on a train in the Middle West and there was this man who was so elegant. He had a very strange accent and he was interested in all kinds of things, like arts. He was the first New Yorker I had ever seen, and it seemed to me very glamorous. I had a play done as soon as I came here, so I was caught up at once in that sort of glamour side of New York, and that made the scene even more exciting to me.

Upper West Side

180° horizontal view: Broadway at 76th Street, looking east.

Upper West Side

Upper West Side

If I have to say what I like about New York, mainly I like my friends—after all, I have been here fifteen years. I think a lot of people will quote the plays and the museums and so on; but if you ask them how often do they really go to them, it wouldn't be so many times. Though I do go probably more than most people. But I think what I really like is the fine range of people, and what they're talking about, and their life styles. A lot of people who don't really even like New York—it's too noisy, too dirty, too competitive and so on—come here because they were too strange to fit into their local community. That's true for gay people, but it's true for all—I mean, there are a lot of freaks in New York.

Another thing I like very much is that you go out and you see people. I like to see people, pedestrians. New York is really a very small city in that sense. I mean, Manhattan is very concentrated, you can walk everywhere. Also every New Yorker looks at you and you always look at them, and that's very unusual. In the Middle West people are so polite and so inhibited that they never look at each other at all, it's considered very rude. New York rudeness I find wonderful and a great relief because I was brought up in that very polite Middle Western way.

I think I really am a very typical New Yorker by now in many ways. I am always in a hurry, I have too many things to do. I like that something is happening all the time, and particularly at night because I have a hard time going to sleep. Now in the gay scene the dance bars don't even open until midnight. The Jewish thing is a very important aspect of New York. When I was growing up it was very rare to meet Jews, and a lot of my enjoyment of New York is coming to know them. Of course you can't generalize, but still there are certain traits, like a very funny, a very earthy sense of humor, a great respect for intelligence, and a lot of interest in theater and show business and in the arts.

To me the city seems very poetic. Even though you never see the ocean, you can often smell it in the air. I often have the feeling of all New York being a big sailing ship that is just straining at the anchor and ready to go to sea. It hasn't quite decided whether to be part of America, whether to be part of Europe, or maybe to be its own country altogether, and it's about to take off, it's about to go somewhere.

In New York I think there is the real space that the people have created themselves in a very unplanned way, like in Greenwich Village, which is the kind I like. Then there is the kind of space that has been created on Sixth Avenue by architects and designers, which I hate. You feel like a little tiny lost ant crawling across one of those plazas, freezing in winter, boiling in summer. They are strictly kind of mausoleums for office workers in the day time and they're deserted at night. I worked there. It's terrible. You look out your little window, and you can't open it. Every floor is identical to every other. And you feel so detached from other people and from anything real.

Columbus Avenue at 86th Street, looking south.

Morningside Heights and Harlem

360° horizontal view: Irvin's office, window towards east.

Irvin

36, computer researcher; born New York City; lives on Morningside Drive.

This is Morningside Heights, the upper West Side of Manhattan, and I live here because I work at Columbia University. This whole neighborhood is dominated by the university and some other institutions, which in a sense keeps it from being integrated with the poor neighborhood around it. There's Harlem on the east; on the north is a large immigrant neighborhood which now I think is mainly Puerto Ricans; and the same thing could probably be said for the area on the south. I always call it Fortress Columbia because that's sort of what it's like. I live in one of the buildings owned by the university, and right now it's only for university people.

I write computer programs to allow biologists and chemists to look at nerve cells in three dimensions. When I enter my laboratory I enter a strange world of machines. The computers have a funny effect on me. I get sort of wound up with the machines and they are very intense. I can sit at one of those terminals—they look something like a television screen—for ten or fifteen hours without losing touch with the machine.

I am sort of an intense person and very affected by people around me; the city is too intense for me and makes me more intense. That's why I don't like New York. I need a place that allows me to settle down, that doesn't have so much interaction. The whole city is too intense, too much activity. All of that stuff becomes distractions that I have to shield myself from, and that takes energy from me. I also don't like the crowding. I just like to have natural scenery around me. All these buildings make me feel claustrophobic and crowded.

Morningside Heights and Harlem

300° horizontal view: Morningside Drive at 116th Street, towards west.

I try to be very keenly aware of what's happening around me, more often almost at a subconscious level. I guess growing up as a New Yorker you sort of become street wise, you know, always watching out for dangerous situations and incidents. In fact I tend to avoid people; especially around this neighborhood, there is this feeling of running into bums or muggers or crazies. It's not so much a feeling of fear, it's a feeling of defensiveness: I just take a very defensive stand when I am in the city. Which is another thing I don't like about it. My feeling about New York is that it's a giant hill with people crawling all over each other, and cars and noise.

I lived six years in Boston and seven years in California, and in neither of those places did I ever have that kind of tension. My image of the change in going from New York to California is of going from one place where people communicate intensely to a place that is essentially a communication vacuum. People there live in suburbia, at large distances from each other, and they travel around in cars like little bubbles. They're isolated from each other, they don't interact with other people. They have to learn to deal with their own inside—which I never had the chance to, because in New York I was so bombarded with stimuli that I was never able to get directly in touch with my own guts in a self-aware way. And that's what made me see a psychiatrist.

Morningside Heights and Harlem

I remember one night going out on a mountain ridge and looking down with this friend of mine at this expanse of the San Francisco bay, and my friend said to me, "When you are not feeling good in California, the nice thing to know is that nature is on your side." In New York, if you're not feeling good, the city can be incredibly oppressive, because it's not nature, it's unnatural, all this crowding and intensity and pressure. Here, when I want to relax, I go indoors to shield myself from all the intensity and the noise and the dirt. In California, when I want to relax, I go outdoors because it's beautiful and you can just live out in the open.

I grew up in a white middle-class Jewish family. I think the fact that they were middle class is more important than their ethnic origins. We lived in the Bronx, in Brooklyn, and in Forest Hills in Queens. There are a lot of things about being a real New Yorker that I just don't like—a kind of provincialism and chauvinism, the attitude that all other people are sort of dumb and stupid. I have a couple of sisters and brothers-in-law who are, I would say, very provincial New Yorkers. They can't identify with other people, they really see the world through a set of New York glasses.

Morningside Heights and Harlem

Looking east at Morningside Drive at 116th Street: trees
of Morningside Park, buildings in Harlem.

Harlem from a roof at 119th Street. ▷

Sylvia

21, student; born in Harlem; lives in Harlem.

I grew up in Harlem, then I went to the Bronx, then I moved back to Harlem, on the West Side, 115th Street and St. Nicholas. The neighborhood is rather worn down, it has a lot of old buildings. The streets, like all streets in Harlem, are very dirty most of the time. But now they got this thing where the people who live there do the cleaning of the streets, because the garbage men don't come around very often, and when they do they just throw the garbage all over the place. They just leave it there, and the people that sweep the streets just come around once in a while. So now the people in the neighborhood do most of the sweeping; they got a community thing.

There's plenty of stores around. The prices in Harlem are higher because there's a lot of robberies, a lot of the trucks get robbed, so the prices are going up. A lot of people say Harlem is much wilder than Brooklyn or Queens or places like that. I don't think so. I guess that's because I was raised in Harlem, you know. They say that there are a lot of junkies, they say you get robbed. But I don't know. I used to work at a restaurant and I didn't get home until 1:30 at night and I came by myself and I have never been robbed or raped or anything like that in Harlem. And when I was going to high school I used to have to be there at 7:40. So I would leave my house at seven and I used to walk to 110th Street. There used to be a lot of junkies and winos in the streets, and they would say hello, good morning, and I would speak to them. They didn't bother me. It's just the fact that when I passed I didn't treat them like garbage. So I would say Harlem was a nice place to be raised and live, if you just go about your own business. There are certain people you do communicate with, there are certain people you don't communicate with. If you pick your friends, the ones you want to be with, it's not much trouble.

Harlem is a nice place to have fun because there's so many different places you can go to. There's a lot of clubs and a lot of discos, things like that, and a lot of bars that you can go into that are really rowdy, if you know where you're going. You have a lot of restaurants around—Chinese restaurants, Muslim restaurants. And we have the Muslim temple.

In this neighborhood there's not many Puerto Ricans, hardly any whites. They come once in a while, but most of the time when the white people come they're just selling drugs or something like that. A Yellow Cab won't come into the neighborhood because they have been robbed so many times. You find prostitutes on 115th Street and Eighth Avenue, they will be up there; but on 115th Street and Lenox Avenue there's not many prostitutes. A lot of drug addicts and pushers, you know, and a lot of big fancy cars, a lot of people dressing fancy, but that's all it is—fancy cars, a lot of fancy talk, and that's about it. There's not many rapes on that block, you know.

People die in Harlem over stupid things, like accidents. And a lot of people have big ideas and, like in any other borough, they figure that drugs is the quickest way to get to the big ideas. A lot of them get into it and find out it's not worth it and most of them—eight out of ten times—get out of it before they are in too far.

Everybody that I know in my neighborhood, they do go to school. You have those that don't, but most of them do go to school. There's a lot of young girls that are pregnant (at fifteen, sixteen) that have had kids—some two, some one. And there's a lot of alcoholics—kids. They get out in the streets because there is nothing at home for them, and a lot of them leave home at an early age. Just the usual problems that you might hear about in all the boroughs, but since Harlem is so big you hear about problems there more than you do in any other borough. So many more people come to Harlem, a lot of people from the south, a lot of people from the West Indies. When they come, they come straight to Harlem. So it's really overcrowded, you know, there are a lot of people there.

The building I live in, like it was going bad and we couldn't get the landlord to do anything with it. All he wants you to do is pay your rent. The boiler was broken most of the time, the elevator was broken most of the time, and the lights. Last summer, all the lights in the building were turned out, the ones that the landlord had to pay for—he owed them six thousand bucks and he didn't want to pay them. So now the people own the building, we don't have any landlords. And the tenants got a lawyer for the building. They put the rent money in the bank and pay the bills for what needs to be fixed with the money they have in the bank.

We have a lot of old people that have been living there for thirty, twenty-five years. They live on the top floors and when the elevator is broken they have to walk up. Like when they turned out the lights in our building, somebody would always be downstairs. When old people come in we go upstairs with them, so nobody will get robbed, so they won't get hurt going up steps by themselves. A lot of people say that people in Harlem are all for themselves, but you can find people that help each other. Like in our building, one time the water pump broke and we would help the old people take water to the fifth floor, the seventh floor.

When I was younger we didn't have anything like a community center. Then when I was around fifteen, in this building at 114th Street and St. Nicholas there was an empty basement. So what we did, we made our own community center, you know, to keep the kids off the streets. We would have parties down there, we would do things like sing and we would make up different groups, and we kept a lot of kids off the streets. So we did things to help ourselves. And the church right next door to where I live came out

Harlem from a roof at 119th Street. ▷

with a community thing. We used to go down there and we had African dances, African drums, literature, things like that, poetry, you know. You could go in there—it was free—and they would have an instructor. And one summer we went to Green Haven prison and we did a show for them up there. Just a lot of things to keep you busy in Harlem. For me, it's a nice neighborhood to be raised.

Buses are close, the train is close, shopping centers are close. If you want to go and buy clothes, you can walk to 115th Street. In the summer time I like to walk slow. In the winter I walk fast because it's cold. In Harlem you look out, you know, because you don't want to get in a crowd where they're fighting. You can look up a block and you can tell if something is happening just by the way people are crowded on the street. I don't know—instinct.

I went to Rochester and I liked it there for the living conditions. There wasn't so much you could do for recreation, but the buildings were lower, the air was much cleaner, there wasn't so much fog, smoke, and smelliness in the air. So I was impressed by the low buildings in Rochester more than I am by the high buildings in Harlem. I can't really imagine why they want to build them so tall. Because, you know, when the elevator breaks, people live on the twenty-seventh floor, how are they going to walk up twenty-seven flights? I can't understand why they want the buildings to be so tall. A lot of people say that they try to reach the impossible, you know, try to reach past the sky. And I believe it, because every time I turn around the buildings are getting higher and higher.

I feel that Manhattan is the place that you can learn whatever it is you want to learn. I have learned about the city, about people, about just dealing with anything. Because most of the problems you usually have to face are right here already: money shortage, shortage of jobs, trying to survive, just trying to make through one day without getting hurt. You can go to other places to see how other people do whatever it is they do, but most of the time you can learn it right here.

A lot of people from other cities come here to New York, so there's really a mixture of different people, of different cities. And I suppose we have a different language between the boroughs. We have different life styles—I know that. There's a dance called the Hustle. Now the people in Harlem do the Hustle different from the people in Brooklyn, and the people in Brooklyn do the Hustle different from the people in the Bronx. So the Hustle between all these boroughs is done about a hundred different ways: one dance, one step, but it's done so many different ways.

There's bad things about Manhattan too. Drug addicts, you know. The place is dirty most of the time. Killing. And everybody is talking about doing and nobody is doing. Jobs, no way to get jobs. A lot of people are on public assistance. They have lost their jobs and that's the only way they can support themselves. And when they go there, they treat them like, well—that's

Morningside Heights and Harlem

tough, it's just too bad you can't find a job. And then if you start stealing, you go to jail, you know. So what else to do? You're treated like dirt no matter what you do, most of the time. You have to really scuffle and step on a lot of people. The whole city to me is one big plastic bubble. It's transparent, you can see right through it, there's nothing solid. Because everything is a front for something else; people use people to get what they want. If you sit down and look, you can see that there's nothing but lying.

Space is room. Because, you know, Harlem is so crowded. There's so many people, it's hard to get away by yourself. A lot of people I see on the TV, they get up and say, "Well, I want to be by myself," they go in their room and shut the door, and they are by themselves. But me and my sister share a room. You can't really go to the park and be by yourself because there are so many people there. You can't go to a bar and be by yourself because the first thing they're going to think is you're a hooker and you're trying to be picked up. You can't go to a disco by yourself because if you're going home by yourself you're scared somebody will try to rob you, rape you, or something. Space to me is just being somewhere where I can be totally alone when I want to be. There's not much space here to get away by yourself, so you have to make up for that space in your mind. Like a lot of times I can be sitting with a crowd of people around me, but if I don't want to be there I don't have to be there. I just think about being somewhere else. If I want to be alone, I just escape in my mind.

Morningside Heights and Harlem

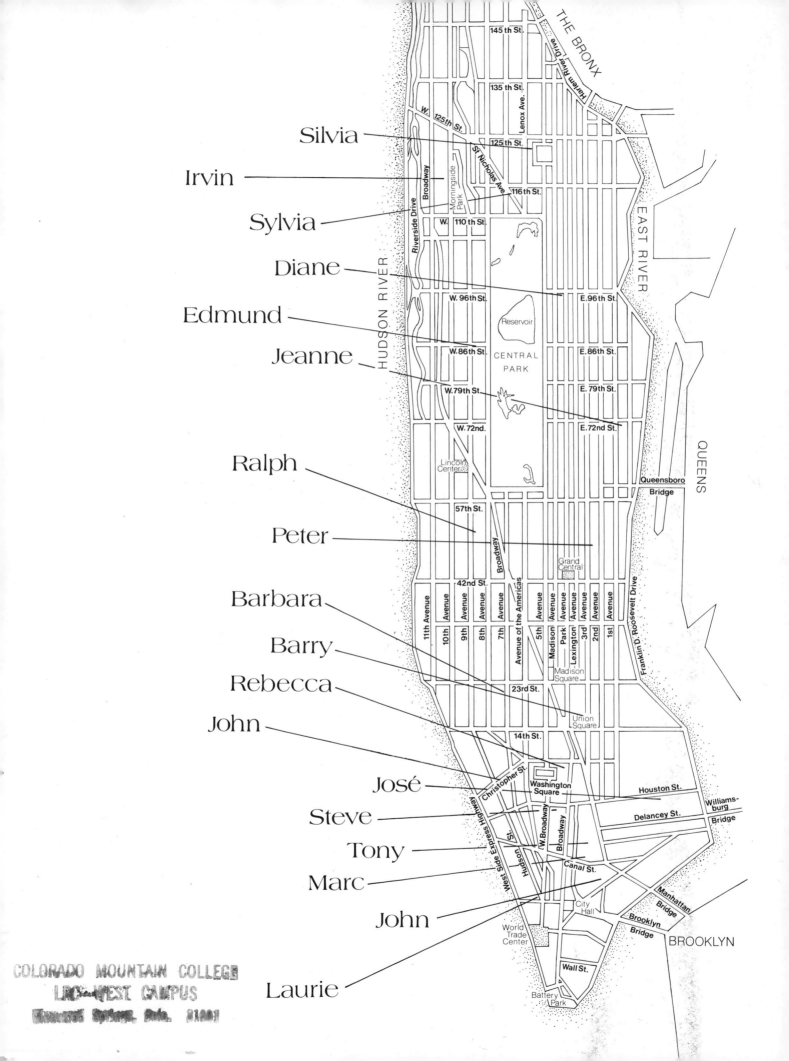

Silvia

Irvin

Sylvia

Diane

Edmund

Jeanne

Ralph

Peter

Barbara

Barry

Rebecca

John

José

Steve

Tony

Marc

John

Laurie

THE BRONX

145th St.

135th St.

W. 125th St.

125th St.

116th St.

W. 110th St.

W. 96th St.

E. 96th St.

W. 86th St.

E. 86th St.

W. 79th St.

E. 79th St.

W. 72nd.

E. 72nd St.

57th St.

42nd St.

23rd St.

14th St.

Houston St.

Delancey St.

Canal St.

Wall St.

Lenox Ave.

Harlem River Drive

St Nicholas Ave.

Morningside Park

Broadway

Riverside Drive

HUDSON RIVER

EAST RIVER

Reservoir

CENTRAL PARK

Lincoln Center

Broadway

QUEENS

Queensboro Bridge

Grand Central

11th Avenue

10th Avenue

9th Avenue

8th Avenue

7th Avenue

Avenue of the Americas

5th Avenue

Madison Avenue

Park Avenue

Lexington Avenue

3rd Avenue

2nd Avenue

1st Avenue

Franklin D. Roosevelt Drive

Madison Square

Union Square

Washington Square

Christopher St.

West Side Express Highway

Hudson St.

W. Broadway

Broadway

Williamsburg Bridge

Manhattan Bridge

Brooklyn Bridge

BROOKLYN

City Hall

World Trade Center

Battery Park